TALK ABOUT DRIVING!

Heather was encouraged to write about her driving by friends and family. Heather is married with three sons and she dedicates this book to the four men in her life and to all women drivers everywhere. She also would like to pay her respects to all the cars she has written off and to give apologies to all those drivers she has confused and stunned by her driving capabilities.

TALK ABOUT DRIVING!

Heather Baber

TALK ABOUT DRIVING!

Olympia Publishers
London

www.olympiapublishers.com
OLYMPIA PAPERBACK EDITION

Copyright © Heather Baber 2011

The right of Heather Baber to be identified as author of
this work has been asserted in accordance with sections 77 and 78 of the
Copyright, Designs and Patents Act 1988.

All Rights Reserved

No reproduction, copy or transmission of this publication
may be made without written permission.
No paragraph of this publication may be reproduced,
copied or transmitted save with the written permission of the publisher, or
in accordance with the provisions
of the Copyright Act 1956 (as amended).

Any person who commits any unauthorised act in relation to
this publication may be liable to criminal
prosecution and civil claims for damage.

A CIP catalogue record for this title is
available from the British Library.

ISBN: 978-1-84897-134-9

This is a work of fiction.
Names, characters, places and incidents originate from the writer's
imagination. Any resemblance to actual persons, living or dead, is purely
coincidental.

First Published in 2011

Olympia Publishers
60 Cannon Street
London
EC4N 6NP

Printed in Great Britain

Contents

When push came to shove 11

More questions than answers 20

Conjecture versus proof 22

A year (or more) in the life of a Driving Instructor 38

Wow! She's the best 54

Driving test success 59

Help! I'm on the road and on my own! 65

No escape – fate dealt me the joker 73

Oh no, not again! 87

You can't argue with a hunt 91

The parting of the ways 96

When push came to shove

Have you ever heard of Genevra Mudge? Perhaps you have, perhaps you haven't.

But what is so incredible is that she hit the headlines over 100 years ago just because she drove a car. Her record was set way back in 1899 and she probably thought then that her achievement would mean that quite soon hundreds of women would be following her lead. Sitting in the driving seat and enjoying the sport of driving.

Wrong!

The fame she had at that time was not only due to her driving, but more importantly because she was a woman.

Genevra had done the unthinkable, she had broken into the sport of driving, which, at that time was for men and considered for men only.

Let's face it, to try and compete in any sport isn't easy, but if you are a woman as well, life is tough! What about the sports of rugby, football, cricket? All male dominated but women are getting there. There are very few sports now which are just for males.

O.K., so women now have world recognition in most sports but how hard has it been for them to get this far? Especially in the car world. It's definitely been an uphill struggle.

There's had to be a lot of pushing, and striving to get themselves recognised as equal drivers to men.

It hasn't been a few years, it hasn't been a few decades but we are now into the 21st century and at last, at long last, most men concede that women can drive as well as them. But what a battle women have fought!

Men may ridicule women for taking so long to get what they wanted, but men have stood shoulder to shoulder on this one.

Over the past 40–50 years their attitude, together with women's self belief has meant that there has been an enormous change towards the equality of women drivers.

Going back to Genevra, if she was in a reality T.V. show to day, she would certainly get the public vote because not only could she show off her driving skills but she would also be able to show how she could cope with those vintage cars which were heavy and cumbersome.

How would you like to start your car by using a heavy metal crank? No gentle turn of a key. Oh no!

Would you have the Herculean strength to pick up the crank, insert it into the front of the car and then manually have to turn it several times so that the engine could be revved up and the gear wheels were then set in motion? I thought not.

Can you imagine the excitement that gripped all drivers when suddenly the crank was obsolete? Suddenly arm muscles were having a holiday! An electric starting handle had been invented. This was in 1910 and this simple addition was being fitted to all of the new models. It certainly made life a bit easier for the few women who were driving, but let's face it; it also helped the many male drivers. Titan body builders were in short supply!

We can give credit to Genevra and all her followers for being able to manage all of this technical stuff, but this was nothing compared to the social problems that women had to overcome during the first half of the 20th Century.

Heavy and cumbersome cars were nothing when compared to the alienation of women in society because of the class system. A society which was made up of upper, middle and lower classes and the status of the very rich was pretty much accepted by the very poor.

Life in the poverty lane was tough.

Benefits? What were they? Help from the Government was non-existent.

The only handouts for the poor were usually from their rich employers, who would condescendingly hand out scraps of food, but the idea of giving extra money didn't seem to be the fashion! The meagre wages that were paid out were considered adequate and asking for a pay rise would be like Oliver Twist asking for 'More'!

It doesn't take much imagination to work out that the aim of the lower class was to survive and the only aim of the upper class was to play!

So it is not surprising that any woman who drove would be part of the wealthy upper class.

It was considered a 'fun activity' for the affluent. The very idea that the 'servants' or 'farm workers' (male or female) would be able to drive was beyond belief.

No one thought that this snobbish attitude would ever be changed. But change it did and pretty dramatically. The 1st World War erupted, the men were sent overseas to fight for their country and all women, not just the rich, but every woman who was physically able, drove.

Women had to become essential drivers. There was no choice. And women showed just how capable they were.

Driving?

A man's job? A rich person's job? Huh.

So what was considered 'a man's job' became a 'woman's job'. Tractors, cars. Nothing was too difficult.

No driving test was needed. Just get behind the wheel girl and drive!

Men weren't around to criticise them. Hallelujah, women were flying high! They knew that their country was in need of them and the tenacity of women was on red alert! We take for granted the successful equality in our modern life, but perhaps, historically, could 1918 be when the seed of equality in driving was sown?

Any, and every type of transport had to be driven, from cars to heavy army lorries and what was considered impossible in previous years, now became the normality.

Women were at the wheel everywhere.

Then the bubble burst. Thankfully the war ended and the men came home. The whole country celebrated at first but then reality clicked in. Men now needed to have a job.

Where could they find work? What could they do?

It was pretty obvious that women would have to "take a back seat" as far as driving was concerned.

Men desperately needed to take up their old jobs and become once again the 'breadwinner' for the family. The old rules of living took over. Men had their roles, women had theirs. The classes drifted back into upper, middle and lower, and the idea of women driving drifted into the clouds of time.

Women, apart from those in the upper classes, went back to being housekeepers. Busy with their home chores, the memories of being important drivers faded and life took over. Once again driving became an occupation for the more affluent but it still wasn't all that acceptable as a genteel occupation, even for those who could afford it.

Cars in the early 1900's didn't particularly lend themselves to feminine fashion. The heavy cars were mostly open topped and girls driving them (or even as passengers) would get windswept and dirty. Such unrefined behaviour was definitely not what…

Mamma would allow!

Then there was the question of maintenance – this was definitively not a job for female hands (or males' come to that) and so mechanics' had to be employed. Yet another reason why cars were owned and driven by the rich.

Of course, on that basis, all drivers' now must be very rich as 99% of us have our cars serviced and repaired by mechanics!

Twenty years raced by before women were once again hurled into the driving picture.

Sadly, it was again due to a War, this time the 2nd World War. So was history going to be repeated and were women going to be back in the 'driving seat'? Of course they were.

Women were elevated again to the position of 'essential drivers'.

Driving became classless. Background didn't make any difference.

From Royalty down to the lower classes women drivers were again needed to help with the war effort

Women were at the wheel. A new generation of women, but just as capable as their mothers had been.

Young women Bus drivers, tank drivers, official chauffeurs, army lorries, anything that needed to be driven, women were there. Competent and clever. Willing and able. Even learning basic mechanics wasn't beyond their capability. But when this war thankfully came to an end, these young women adopted a different attitude.

Freedom was infectious and wasn't going to be given up without a fight. Men had fought on the battle fields, but now the 'little woman' was not content to sit back and be just a housewife.

There was more to the female mind than that, thank you very much.

That little seed of equality was sprouting. It had to be nurtured and although a bit weak, it was there. A foundation of things yet to come.

The ending of this war then didn't mean that driving was only for the rich because, as figures from 1940 – 1970 show, the number of women drivers actually doubled, which probably didn't please the males.

After all, the 'stereotyping' of women driving badly couldn't be thought of as a female idea, could it?

It was pretty difficult for women to cope with the sniggers and snide comments made by men about females at the driving wheel but, thank goodness, many women ignored them and those early shoots grew into strong stems of confidence.

How many years has it taken though? From 1944 when the war ended right up to the new millennium.

What a struggle! But now it's almost over. Women have proven that they can drive as well as men, even though there are still a few chauvinistic males around who have yet to be converted.

In fact most insurance companies these days are prepared to arrange special deals for women drivers as they are considered to be such a low risk.

So women have to be admired for the stoicism, their tenacity, and their self-belief at achieving their aim, which was of course, Equality with driving.

There have been so many women who have staunchly defended their ability to drive. They have battled bravely against so many obstacles and I have so much admiration for all that they have achieved but it doesn't alter the fact that I am not one of them.

A lost cause to the skill of driving.

I know that I have let the side down badly and given men the opportunity to smirk and criticize women's driving. But apologies are not enough. My penitence is not enough.

I can imagine those early pioneers, volcanic in their fury, wanting to erupt their grievance on me with their own design of a stigmata.

In all fairness to myself though, I do believe (well I have to) that there are other women like myself who cannot grasp the idea that a box on wheels can actually be controlled by their own feet and hands. Aren't there?

I apologise for creating the impression that the female mind is not capable of being in control of anything mechanical. It is.

Haven't those woman drivers over the past decades demonstrated all their driving skills?

Yes, they have, of course they have.

But me? Not a chance.

To put it quite simply, I don't like driving.

This is not a petulant, stamp my feet, sort of remark.

It is a fact. Driving and I are just not compatible.

Why? The answer to that is quite simple, I don't understand cars, never will understand them, and really don't want to understand them. When I am in the driving seat I still think of the vehicle as a petrol-consuming box on wheels that won't do as I ask. But when I am a passenger then that is a different story. Then the beast is a purring, comfortable place to be in and I can sit back in luxury and arrive at any destination I have chosen. (Well, as long as the driver, usually my husband, chooses the same place!)

I did try to join the driving elite but as you will learn, trying was one thing, but doing it was another. Even though I did my best and tried to be the crème-de-la-crème, it didn't matter. In the end my love affair with driving just didn't work out. I really did try and nurture our relationship, but we just couldn't bond.

I wasn't on the same wave length at all.

No matter what emotion I chose, tears, smiles, anger, nothing seemed to endear us to each other and after several years we both admitted that parting was the only option.

Without any regrets on either side, in fact we are still the best of friends as long as I am not behind the wheel.

My love affair with cars wasn't a young, passionate fling. The affinity between us began when I was a mature woman. It certainly wasn't love at first sight, more a question of an acceptable arrangement. My need to travel versus the car's need of guidance and companionship.

So, the liaison between us began with me, a mature woman, and a young car eager to please. We both found our first date to be traumatic, but neither of us would admit that we were just on different wave lengths I was too set in my role as a passenger and the engine I was involved with needed an ardent partner.

A partner who would take risks, give guidance, and treat driving with such respect that all journeys would be euphoric!

With me at the wheel, such a partnership was unthinkable.

Our relationship was doomed.

I had several flings but all of the cars felt the same. Gradually, I realised that cars and I would never be compatible.

Perhaps I tried too hard.

I had to face the fact that I was only passenger material.

Genevra Mudge and I do have one thing in common though. We are both teachers. She has taught women that anything can be achieved if you try hard enough, and I can teach women that if you try hard enough you still may not achieve!

But one achievement of hers that women shouldn't go for, is her record of being the first American woman to have an automobile accident.

Genevra Mudge, you should be ashamed of yourself.

In a race meet in New York, you knocked down 5, yes 5 innocent bystanders!

I'm sure you didn't try to achieve this record.

In comparison to me though, because I didn't knock anyone down is not an achievement it's a miracle

More questions than answers

Set in my ways.

Thinking that learning to drive would be easy.

All of my friends could do it, why couldn't I?

O.K. I admit to having many problems but surely there's an answer as to why I have managed to get myself into so many scrapes?

Why haven't I been able to master the art of driving and build up a rapport with any of my cars?

Did I leave it too late to learn to drive?

Possibly, but there are learner drivers who are much older than I was when I was learning and they seem to manage the whole car thing without any problems.

So that can't be a reason.

Could I be suffering from some rare syndrome, yet to be discovered by medical science?

A syndrome preventing some people from developing into competent drivers? A phobia of steering wheels perhaps?

After all there is a phobia of speed – tacophobia and a phobia of trains – siderodromophobia so, surely, if I tried hard enough and persuaded enough people in the medical profession to listen and to examine my fears, surely they could be persuaded that such a phobia exists without deciding that I am completely loopy!

Age, phobia? Weak excuses.

So how about the effects of driving during my childhood. Instead of a psychiatrist perhaps I should be interviewed by a psychologist .

So, three tries to sort my manic driving out.

Age.

Medical.

Childhood depravity.

If any of those could prove why I am so hopeless then I could be what every woman loves to be.

Right!

From these pathetic tries though, the only one that would be worth following I think would be the last one.

Perhaps it should be signposted 'conditioning' as it will probably veer off in so many directions.

A myriad of lanes, all leading to the final destination of 'Hopeless Driver.'

By trying that route I will have to cover every single life experience with cars, but it may, just may, show clearly why I was never destined to be a dab hand behind the wheel.

Conjecture versus proof

Today's children practically live in cars.

It is the normal way of life for most kids.

Their 'chauffeurs' at the wheel, the kids are taken to school, to numerous leisure activities, away on holidays, the list of places to be driven is practically endless.

The idea of walking to and from school has been a no-no for many children, but now the trend is to keep them fit and beat the obesity culture, so walking is becoming a fashion. Feet are being used, shoes are being worn out, and pavements are being pounded once again.

That doesn't mean that cars are becoming extinct though.

That piece of machinery which is parked outside so many houses is still an essential piece of equipment for a lot of families. So essential in fact, that not only one, but often several cars are 'needed'.

How do we manage without them?

How would life go on?

The same as it did not that long ago. Less than 40 years in fact.

Was it only in the '60's that all women were given the chance to be part owner of a car?

So, which car generation are you?

The one with childhood memories of cars.

Or the generation of the liberation for women to drive.

Or the generation of life as we now know it, cars, cars, and more cars!

Personally, I am a mixture of all three.

I am of the second choice, but have a smattering of the first generation and am part of the third!

My 'life with cars' began with deprivation, developed into a desire to drive one, and ends with life as we now know it. Cars, cars and more cars.

None of them driven by me!

If I use my 'deprived childhood experiences' as a reason for being a hopeless driver, then I'll need to go back to my 'smattering' of childhood memories of a world without cars.

I was born on an island. The beautiful Isle of Arran, just off the western coast of Scotland.

Although not that long ago, give or take a decade or two, the sight of a car on the one main road across the island was enough to have all the islanders out staring in disbelief.

The very first car that arrived on Arran was on the Clyde steamer, in 1897!

Way before I was born.

It was brought over for just one tourist. Obviously, one who was pretty rich.

It certainly was not for general use. And, of course, driven by a man.

Tractors and farm machinery were brought over on those sleek steamers and possibly motor bikes, but it wasn't until the 1900's when the tourists began to arrive, those Charabancs full of excited holiday makers were brought to the island.

For those who haven't a clue what a Charabanc is, it is a sort of coach.

At that time driven of course, by a man!

Arran became THE holiday place for the mainlanders.

(Note, again, before I was born.)

Even when the island became an important Naval Base during the Second World War, transport was only by service vehicles.

So that's a great start.

No cars around at my birth.

I'm not old enough to have been driven around in the first car way back in 1897, and the car ferry from the mainland didn't come into service until 1953, so my arrival didn't exactly coincide with some sort of knock-on effect of a car boom.

As well as cars being scarce, there was also the problem of birth facilities. The local hospital didn't have a maternity ward.

No cars and no hospital, there wasn't any choice. I had to be born at home.

Now, here's a puzzle. If the local hospital did have a maternity ward, and if I had been born there then how would I have been taken home?

With few cars on the island my mother would have had to ride on the back of a tractor, carrying me in her arms, and what mother really wants her new baby smelling of a farm yard?

What a start in life. No cosy car seat to snuggle into. No quick drive from maternity ward to home.

A non-car start in my life.

Surely this could be a starting point for one of those lanes that would take me to the final stage of Hopeless Driver?

A psychological reason for my later dislike of driving?

Is it even worth considering?

I'm on a roll now. I need to carry on a bit more.

For several months after my birth I travelled with my mother to quite a few towns in the U.K. As my father was serving in the Navy she wanted to be with him as much as possible. The idea of a motorway was not even a pin prick in anyone's imagination Cars zooming along at over 70 mph on boring tarmac was a thing of the future.

Speedometers would scarcely have reached 40 mph! That was fast!

The only way we could reach that sort of speed was by train. No one had a choice. A classic case of train tracks versus walking and the tracks won. Everyone travelled by rail. Platforms were never empty. Standing on crowded platforms was quite normal and there wasn't any choice. Hundreds of people standing shoulder to shoulder, craning their necks to watch for the tendrils of smoke. Eager to hear the loud whistle as the huge dragon of an engine roared into its lair, waiting hungrily to devour its huge meal of coal. It would stand at the pump as if it was waiting for a pint of beer.

This was the age of the steam train. Dirty, smelly engines, chugging slowly all over the country. Engine drivers pulling at levers to let out the steam and clog everyone's lungs up with the gritty vapour.

Men in filthy overalls, black sooty faces and not a woman anywhere to be found in the engine cabs!

The smell of the steam was hated by so many people but I loved it. The fumy smell of petrol will never have the same effect. The effect of water on hot coals is the eau-de-cologne of vehicle vapours to me.

So, train travel is another reason for my 'depravity' about cars and driving.

Kids will find this quite unbelievable but cars didn't play a part in my early travelling.

More deprivation then?

After all the steam engine was running right up until 1966 and we all used it.

Cars will never take the place of my beloved steam train. With that bit of machinery I did have a love affair. Loyal as I am, I still do!

So could this really be another psychological breakthrough?

Adoration of steam and heavy metal versus petrol and rubber tyres?

My memories of steam trains are one thing though, trying to get to grips with my attitude toward cars is another.

Moving on with my personal reminiscences' I am going to try at yet another break through.

A fact that will get kids' minds whirling.

Parents didn't drive themselves to work, or catch a fast diesel/electric train.

My Dad worked in the dockyard and caught the 'docker's bus' and that was the example of parents' travelling to work that we had.

Morning and evening, the dirty buses took the men to work.

These buses were for the workers only. The seats were greasy and black from the dockers' overalls, and the air was thick with the smoke from their cigarettes.

No woman in their right mind would want to drive such a disgusting vehicle even if they were allowed to!

At the beginning and end of the working day, the whistle would blow and the men would stream in or out of the dock gates, travelling by bus, bicycles or walking.

No cars.

Definitely no cars.

Own one of those? No chance.

No 'labourer' could afford a luxury like that! It was unheard of.

Doctors or other professionals may have been able to buy one, and of course the wealthy could always own one.

Was it only a few decades ago that not only were there hardly any cars being driven around but roads were hardly being used either.

Children could actually cross one without being afraid of being knocked down!

The only vehicles that were around at that time were mainly vans for delivering groceries. Not a supermarket one delivering shopping ordered from the internet.

No juggernauts tearing around.

Just a small van making its way around the town and villages delivering weekly orders.

How about this phenomenon for the children of today (and their parents come to think) milk was delivered to the door on a milk float. There were dustcarts, and coal lorries.

Fire engines, Ambulances and Police cars. Those were the vehicles being driven then on the narrow roads.

So, with so few vehicles on the roads, were any of them being driven by women?

No way. They were too busy with the housework.

The example set to the children was obvious, boys could be drivers when they grew up but girls could not.

How fair is that?

Even though they had been driving during the second world war, the idea of women driving as a career in the 1950's would ricochet like a leaking balloon.

Am I convincing anyone, apart from myself, how deprived I was of any involvement, experience and general lack of knowledge I had of a car, and women driving?

Were there role models of women drivers? No.

More importantly is all of this a good enough reason for my total dislike of driving which developed many years later? Well, it may have been, but if that is the case then it would have affected most women of that era, wouldn't it.

I was never driven to school by car. My Mum wasn't one of the harassed Mums or Dads waiting to join in the convoy of the 'school run'.

The lack of experience of cars trailed after me right up until I left school.

I wasn't even lucky enough to have a bicycle. Riding one could at least have given me some sort of idea of what to do on a road, like riding on the right side, braking, being in control of wheels, even if it was two and not four. But I never owned one, and have only ever been on one once, fell off, and never sat on a saddle again. One thing I could do though, was ride a horse. I could manage to sit on that saddle and stay on. It didn't help me with gaining any road sense though, as I only rode in fields, and feet in stirrups don't feel the same as feet on pedals. Guiding by reins is much easier than by turning a stupid wheel.

So is my deficiency in understanding anything mechanical, proof or conjecture?

Will this shortage of knowledge show up later in my lack of driving skills?

Skills which I did eventually try to obtain but wasn't exactly in the top bracket!

Surely there's a little glimmer of proof towards my theory of cars influencing my childhood years, isn't there?

I'm trying hard to justify my ineptitude and my pathetic attempts have now reached those years of freedom and progress.

Yes, the early 60's.

This may come as a bit of a shock, but not everyone was affected by all the hype of this era, and the Cornish were in a pleasant time warp.

I left school, I had a job and I walked. Everyone walked everywhere, or rode their bikes.

My first experience of being involved with a motor driven vehicle was the motor bike.

The idea of sitting on the back of a machine which had an engine, moved on two wheels and came with horse power, frightened the daylights out of me. The only way I could be persuaded to get on one, let alone ride on one, was because it meant a close encounter with my current boyfriend. I had to be the passenger of course. No way would a girl be allowed to rev up and drive away on a motor bike!

Gradually I was hooked and I appeared so confident as I stuck to his leather jacket like a burr, pretending that I was actually enjoying the experience! After several trips locally I did begin to enjoy the ride, especially when I realised that I didn't have to do anything. I was only expected to sit and hold him around the waist. Great.

Crash helmets weren't needed and if they had been then that would have been the end of a beautiful relationship. Having one of those stuck on my head? No thanks.

The thrill of being at one with a motor went to my husband's head and it wasn't very long before he bought his first car. He was so proud of it. He tried to impress me with all the knowledge he had about its mechanics, but all I took in was the fact that it was a bright yellow. O.K. that is a woman thing, to notice the colour, but after all these years, I do remember that it was a Triumph Herald and I can even remember it's registration number plate. I can also remember that the trend for young men was vying with each other over the type, age, model of these boxes on four wheels. So what's new? Any young women in this vying mode then? Of course not. How could they, on the wages they earned as secretaries, hairdressers, shop assistants, nurses, etc. Typical jobs for women.

Equality was probably not even a word listed in the Oxford Dictionary.

Women weren't supposed to own cars, they weren't supposed to drive cars. They were just accessories to boost the young men's ego. And I was one of them!

I sat in the passenger seat, not even remotely interested in how the engine sounded or how smooth it was to put in to gear. That stuff was for the boys. Perhaps if I had taken more notice then, I could have done better later in my driving lessons, but all that interested me, way back then, was waving to my friends.

How to control the car?

That was boring.

How fast it could go?

Boring.

Fuel consumption.

Boring.

A monotonous tirade of unimportance in my life.

What I didn't take on board was how important a car was. She was part of our life. (That's another question, why are cars always referred to as 'she's'? Could it be a question of gender control?)

I don't think I ever thought how bad it must have been for my husband to give up his Triumph.

From swanning around in a bright yellow Triumph Herald, we had to down grade to a white van to cope with our growing family. We needed a more practical vehicle. We had kids and a dog.

Not a people carrier, they were yet to be invented. We changed to a van. A van to take the paraphernalia of baby stuff. A van. No longer the trendy saloon, vying with the smart young men. No bright yellow trendsetter. Just a plain old ordinary practical white van.

Did it bother me? Nope.

I was a housewife and my career was being a full time Mum.

I didn't worry if it was a van or a car I was still very happy to be driven around as were most of my friends.

Weren't they?

No, they weren't. The 'age of the '60's had dawned' and suddenly feminism had smoothly infiltrated our lives and women were asking; – "Why not me?"

"Why can't I do that?"

I didn't ask. I wasn't aware that women were driving. I wasn't anxious to edge my way on to the driving seat. Cars, drivers, engines all passed over me like a lazy breeze passing beyond and out of my conscious thoughts.

Car salesmen and advertisers were aware though. They were conscious of women's desires.

They quickly realised that the market was changing and adverts would now have to change from appealing just to men. Instead of using the gimmick of sexy females draping themselves over the bonnet of the latest model, the advertisers' began to catch on to the fact that cars could and would be used by both men and women. The concept took a while though and they hadn't quite realised that women drivers were going to grab a fair chunk of the car market. That chunk was still being taken up by the affluent as there was still the belief that cars were only for the rich. In 1964 an advert in The Guardian showed a picture of the latest Daimler, two children in the back, their well dressed mother by its side and the patronising caption 'Ideal for the little woman to take the children to school in'. So, the sexy symbol had gone but it was being replaced by adverts still patronizing women and the use that a car held for them. But some progress had been made. Women were in the advertisements as drivers and not as show pieces.

In the 1970's, advertisers' began to show both men and women in their campaign. Now they pictured young men and women driving off to ski or in sports cars. Sharing the car. Sharing the experience. Sharing the fun.

Women were being drawn in to this new lifestyle. Driving was now classless and appealing to many women. But not to all, and I was one of those who weren't brainwashed by all this motor hype. No way.

What was a Daimler anyway, and why would any woman want to take the kids to school in a car when they could walk.

No, I was not influenced, by the car, the woman, the children or driving As a non-driver what I did see was the deviousness of men as they persuaded their women to take up another role Like Svengali, a different mode was adopted. Why?

Because men had realised that by encouraging their wives to drive meant that they could drink more and have a taxi service home! Nice thinking guys and the women fell for it.

The trend was set.

Women drove.

Not me!

I was still content to sit in the passenger seat and be ferried around.

So when our eldest son began to take driving lessons, and eventually passed his driving test I was delighted. Delighted that he had passed or delighted that I had another chauffeur?

Then our second son passed his test, so now I had 3 taxi drivers. Life couldn't be better.

No stress, and no need to even think about ever driving myself! Yep, life was great.

Or was it?

All of the women I knew were driving everywhere. Driving to do their shopping, acting as taxi drivers for both husband and children. Driving to the nearest big town or City. Women drove where they wanted to go, and didn't have to wait until their husbands were available to take them. The arguments in their households were about who was to have the car keys and the car itself. Me? I had to argue my case as to where I wanted to go, and why I wanted to go there, and did it have to be that day? In the end the envy I felt as I saw my female friends and relatives enjoying their freedom got to me and I felt that I had no choice but to pluck up the courage and ask my husband if he would teach me. His reaction was just a cold stare and "No".

Well, I had tried, but what a wimp! It just proved how reluctant I really was. If I had really wanted to get behind the wheel I wouldn't have taken that reaction. Oh no!

It took a while but the "Why can't I," "Why not me?" questions were niggling at me.

A bit later than all of my feminist friends but the questions were sneaking their way into my mind. Could I do it?

Yes, I could. (Huh!)

I knew how easily I could be persuaded not to try, so before I faltered from this emerging cocoon of confidence, I phoned a driving school and booked my first driving lesson.

I may give excuses for my driving lessons, I can try explanations, but I know that before long I will have unleashed the anger of both males and females witnessing the dreadful mess I made. The mutterings of "Stupid fool," "How can anyone be as thick as that?" etc. will soon erupt into a torrent of abuse. I admit that I will deserve those comments, but I am sure that there are many women who will sympathise with the efforts I made and recognise their own endeavours. I appeal to all those women who are suffering their own personal terror of being behind the wheel, not to give up. The thought that they can never take, and pass, a driving test is nonsense. I would like to take each learner by the hand, look into their eyes and persuade them that they can do it. They can forget the idea that passing is an impossibility. It isn't. All they have to do is convince themselves of that.

I suppose that the best advice I can give, speaking as an expert of bad driving, is to encourage them to compare my experiences with their own. That will surely give any woman confidence!

But more important than that, I can equally take pride in the fact that I, yes me, passed my driving test first time! How did I do it? I have no idea, but I did.

One thing that is certain about learning to drive is that it isn't geared to any particular age.

16-years-olds through to 50 or even 60-year-olds. The appeal of driving is ageless. The apprehension, though, must be pretty universal. Anyone who is just about to try and master the skill of driving can learn from me, that whatever they do, there is always someone better or worse than they are. (In my case, I've no need to state the obvious,) Learner drivers do need 'that someone' to hold them by the hand, and much as I would like to offer my services, breathing any confidence into any one would really be like the kiss of death.

No, their greatest friend and ally would be their chosen Driving Instructor.

That vanguard of the motoring profession.

How patient do they have to be?

How courageous?

Every day they are putting their lives in the hands of novices, both male and female.

They must be so relieved when their working day is over. (Thinking about that though they must also be a bit masochistic surely. After all, they manage to survive each day with their nerves in tatters, and then go out the next day and do it all over again! And even with the same client!)

To be fair, the Instructors must have to be pretty long-suffering, and at every moment their exasperation has to be kept in check.

Whether male or female, learner drivers have to be put at their ease.

Just like little fledglings, the inexperienced have to be nurtured until they are ready to fly.

Well, drive. But the essence of the young and weak developing into the strong and self-assured is the same.

To sum up then, my experiences will almost certainly anger a few, be a conversation point to many, and give hope to all those aspiring drivers. They can take heart in the knowledge that there is always someone worse than them, and I most certainly am one of those 'someone's'. The ultimate star of manic driving.

A year (or more) in the life of a Driving Instructor

Even manic drivers have to start somewhere, though, and, having booked my first lesson, I was really chuffed with myself and looked forward to being behind the wheel of a car for the first time in my life.

My little red book had arrived. My provisional licence nicely stuck on the back page.

Doesn't it seem weird that in the early nineties our driving licences were little books, with cardboard covers. No photographs for identification, just the licensee's signature.

So, here I was. All set. Legally allowed to drive on the road. Wow!

I never even thought that I wouldn't be able to master the skill of driving.

After all, my husband drove, both of our sons could drive, most of my female friends drove, so how difficult could it be?

I soon found out.

And so did my poor driving instructor, bless him.

The confidence I had when I phoned him for my lessons had been and gone. I was feeling so very sick and I hadn't even got out of bed! This was the start of my longed-for driving and already I was regretting it. Whatever had I been thinking of? Making an impulsive decision like that? Perhaps I could phone him and say I had changed my mind but then everyone would know that I had chickened out. Everyone in the family would laugh at me. No, I had to do it.

Overwrought, jittery are only two of the adjectives I can name of how I felt that day. I paced up and down, checking in the mirror every so often in case I had developed that nervous twitch under my eye that I get when I am nervous.

"Oh, my God he's here."

The car was parked outside, and I was inside. I had to get myself from the house to that damn car and I had to do it with confidence.

I always knew I should have been an actress, because I deserved an Oscar for my performance. At least I think I should, my driving instructor probably could see me for what I was, though. A gibbering wreck of a woman with high hopes of becoming a first class driver.

I wondered if driving instructors had little black books which have the title of "People who shouldn't be allowed on the roads" or something similar.

(I did think 'people' and not 'women') If they have, then how soon do their clients have their names taken? More importantly, would I be one of them?

I had never met my driving instructor before and to protect his sanity and his reputation I haven't any choice but to give him an alias.

Mr. Foster.

We introduced ourselves and I could tell that he would do his best to make me feel relaxed.

He was the ultimate in long suffering. His skills at not showing exasperation were unique.

However it wasn't long before my driving managed to burrow into his personality, leaving behind huge holes of exasperation and patience.

But on this day he had no idea of his future and what I could do!

I got into the passenger seat and off we went. We drove for a while and then he stopped the car and asked me to change places with him and sit in the driver's seat.

As I moved around the car I realised that my escape route was now closed. I should have stopped there, given my apologies and gone home. But no, I was going to do this.

I had never been behind the driving wheel before and already my imagination was soaring. My confidence was back, I was flying with euphoria. How impressed my family would be with me …but my reverie was suddenly interrupted when I heard …'and that's the 4th gear"

"What?"

As any action I take is always preceded by my thoughts, it may be useful to know exactly when I have them which means that I am going to have the embarrassment of having to write '*Thought*,' when it occurred to me. Which was quite frequent because I quickly found out that I was a bit slow at keeping up with all the verbals and most of the time was at a loss for words. But I wasn't at a loss for thoughts. There was a continual battle in my head between the information that was being rapidly thrown at me and my mental images. Added to that was the totally foreign language for my mechanically deprived self to understand.

I so wished I hadn't started this.

"I am so sorry I didn't quite hear what you were saying just then."

"I was taking you through the gears."

Thought – but I am sitting here, you haven't taken me anywhere, the car is stationary.

Very patiently Mr. Foster started again.

"I was explaining that you will need to know all about the gears and the need to change from one to the other."

"Yes?"

This is something I can understand. There is a gear and that changes. Good. Fact learned.

"But first you have to know about the pedals."

Thought – pedals = bicycles – don't they? Help, I can't ride a bike!

"There are 3 pedals and you have to make sure that your foot is on the correct one as you control the car."

"Yes, I understand, and where are they?"

"By your feet."

God, how thick am I. Stop thinking about bicycles and concentrate. You are now in a car.

Mr. Foster gave a big sigh. He is beginning to regret this I am sure and my name will be written down in his little black book perhaps under 'C' for 'clueless', or 'G' for 'gormless'.

"Look at the pedals," He wasn't smiling now.

"I can see them."

"Good. We can call them A, B, and C which is short for Accelerator, Brake and Clutch. Now put your foot on the Accelerator. No that's the Brake. That's it."

Thought – panic, which way does he mean by A, B, C? B is easy, that's the middle pedal, but which way round are the others? Do they go from left to right or right to left? Had he told me this already? Is it A.B.C. or C.B.A

All of this thinking must have taken several seconds with me staring down at my feet and trying to link them in with the semantics of A B C and C B A! To a complete novice like myself I wished that someone had written the "Complete Idiot's Guide to Driving" which I could have read before parking myself in the driving seat of a car and expecting to be taught how to drive!

No good now though I'm here, and getting more and more confused by the second.

"On your left, no left, not right, there is a handbrake. To use this you have to push in the button on the end, like this." Mr. Foster lowered the hand brake.

"Now you try."

By now I was getting a bit flustered and trying perhaps a little bit too hard to concentrate.

I tried to do it just like him, copying him and used my right hand, but found this so difficult.

"Try using your left hand, you won't be able to use your right hand if, by any chance you have to have that hand on the steering wheel" was the cold advice I was given. Whoops!

My name in his little black book would now be in CAPITALS that's for sure. Now I was feeling even more stupid. It's bad enough not knowing you're A. B. C. from your C.B.A. but now I don't know my left hand from my right.

Confusion was now ballooning into panic. Help! Please can I go home now. Now. This very minute.

Deep breathing. Calm. I must stay calm.

I am learning, and just have to remember that I don't have to use exactly the same hand as Mr. Foster. Just because he'd used his right hand for the hand brake release didn't mean that I had to do the same. I had to release it by using my left hand.

Once I grasped that bit of know-how I was O.K.

Thought - I am confused, at a loss for words, not taking anything in, a white-out has me in its grip. Why oh why did I want to do this?

With my left hand I found the button and pulled up the handbrake.

"Good, now release it."

Done.

A simple action but my excitement at getting something right cleared the fog in my head.

Thought – Mr. Foster is a very good instructor, he is galvanising me into action and trying to make me think a bit more positively. And that is not easy at the moment.

"You always have to check your mirrors before you start to drive. Many accidents happen because the driver hasn't checked his mirrors correctly so it is essential that you learn to do this before you start any journey. Before you drive off at any time, check your mirrors. So now, look into the rear view mirror, that one, and check that you can see the road behind. If you can't see it then you have to adjust it to suit your vision. Now check the side mirrors, and again make sure you can see clearly. The next thing to do is to check your seat and adjust it if you have difficulty reaching the pedals."

I had no trouble checking the mirrors.

How do I adjust the seat then? I looked to the left then to the right.

Thought – How does it adjust anyway? Up, down, forward, back?

Being the excellent driving instructor that he was, Mr. Foster must have been watching me very carefully

A slight cough. A clearing of his throat.

"Do you know how to adjust the seat?"

"No." I whimpered.

"The bar to adjust your seat is usually at the front of the seat, at the bottom."

"You will have to …" A pause. "You will have to …" Another pause.

By now I was so curious that he had all my attention. No longer confused or panicking I couldn't take my eyes off him.

This seemed to make matters worse and as he squirmed in his seat I suddenly realised that he was embarrassed.

"Are you O.K., Mr. Foster?"

Another cough, and then he took a deep breath and before he took another one he blurted out: – "To adjust your seat, you have to put your hand between your knees, locate the metal bar and pull it to let your seat go forward."

All the time he was saying this he was sitting like a statue and staring out of the windscreen.

Thought – Oh, you poor man. What an instruction to have to give to a woman.

I didn't dare ask if I should use my right hand or my left.

Gingerly I did as he asked and put my hand (right) between my knees, groped around, and found the metal bar, pulled it and shot forward, knees to steering wheel, hand still caught between my knees.

"I'd advise you to put your seat a bit further back."

How he could keep such a straight face I really don't know.

I gave a deep sigh and in all fairness to myself, the nervous giggle that was building up I did manage to keep under control.

So mirrors have been checked. Seat altered, and at a good position as well.

"Before we start you have to make sure that the car is in neutral."

Thought – Neutral, neutral When was he talking about that? During pedal time? During handbrake time? Neither of those? My head was spinning. I was back again in white-out. Concentrate, come on. Mr. Foster came to my rescue. He'd had enough of the 'hands, knees, and whoops-a-daisy,' bit and was once more in his confident role as my instructor.

"Would you like me to go through the gears again?"

That was it! Slowly my own brain came into its own slow gear. Neutral, first, second, third, and fourth. (Thank goodness there wasn't a fifth back then).

Thought – But how did I get to them? Ah ha – the stick thing. Yes, that's it. The gear stick.

I've remembered. Now I just have to work out how I put all that knowledge into practice I didn't have a clue as to what he had been saying when he explained the gears the first time round.

"Yes, please. I'm still not sure how to go about them."

That sounded good. So intelligent. Shows concentration

"O.K. Place your left foot on the clutch."

Blank stare.

"Pedal C."

Thought – Oh God, not that again.

"Pedal C."

"That's the clutch."

"Correct."

Did he realise that I was playing for time. Gingerly I put my foot on the pedal on the left of the brake and waited. I almost punched the air when his next words were:–

"Now press down on the clutch and at the same time move the gear stick forward, that's first, then right back, that's second gear, now you have to …….wait I'll help."

Mr. Foster put his hand over mine and showed me how to do a funny wiggly thing and then I was apparently in third gear. But could I do it on my own, that is the question? It was quite a while before I was able to understand what he meant by "Back across and up."

With Mr. Foster still guiding my hand we went into fourth gear.

"Now try it on your own."

Crunch.

"And again."

Metallic screech.

Mr. Foster had another go at guiding me so I didn't have any problem. But on my own? Big, big sigh. After several goes (I lost count) I did manage it. I didn't really know how, though, and to expect me to remember something that I hadn't a clue how I had learned in the first place was a bit much.

I never knew for weeks that this car was dual controlled and what I couldn't do, he did.

The morning had been all about panic, confusion, lack of comprehension and so many other emotions. But, and there was a but, it hadn't been a complete waste of my time, I knew I had learned something. What it was I had yet to find out, but there was a tiny spark of, dare I say, hope – or is that being too optimistic.

I felt the morning had been worthwhile even if it had been hard work for both of us.

Gratefully, I turned towards him,

"Thank you so much Mr Foster, I have really enjoyed today and I have learned so much."

Whilst I was saying this my hand was on the car door handle and I was nearly out of the car and making my way around to the passenger seat, breathing a sigh of relief.. I was ready to go home. I had completely forgotten how long a lesson I had booked for, and didn't have a clue at how much time had passed. (No clock on the dashboard).

But that wasn't on Mr. Foster's mind at all. Completely ignoring me, he said;-

"Now we'll start the engine."

"But you're in the passenger seat."

"That's the idea. You are the one learning to drive."

I gave him my brightest smile.

"I'll look forward to that next time."

"No, we are doing it now."

"But I'm only just learning about the controls and things."

"Yes, and now I want you to put it all into practice."

Thought – you might want to but I certainly don't. No one would be safe on the roads with me at the wheel. Now where did that thought come from? I hadn't even been on the roads as a driver? Later I made the big mistake of quoting this thought to my family. They have never let me forget it. It became a mantra with the three of them. It's a man thing to puncture self esteem. A woman would be much more supportive.

Now it was all about using the accelerator (A) and the clutch (C) at the same time, listening to the engine to know when to release the handbrake. If I was in a fog before, I was now in a coma! My feet were doing things that I had no control over.

And, as for the ordeal of listening and what is more, actually hearing, when the clutch should be released and the accelerator took over, well that needed a degree in audiology as far as I was concerned. Where, Oh! where, was that Idiot's Guide to Driving that I had a craving for?

So, with reluctance, I followed his instructions and I drove. About 18 inches (45 cms.)

Stop.

Tried again. Another couple of feet. That's an improvement then I don't know which was more clenched, my white knuckles on the steering wheel, my buttocks, or my teeth!

That Kangaroo that all learner drivers talk about had appeared and was sitting there, hands over his eyes and moaning. Or was that me?

Not only did I need a complete massage, I also needed to break out of that damn animal's skin!

Slowly, very slowly, I managed to drive or rather lurch and lunge around the back roads and at last we came to the hill leading up to our house. As we approached it I was told to signal that I was turning right and then accelerate the engine a little in order to take the climb. I had forgotten all about how to signal, and to me it was of little concern. All I wanted to do was to get home. As soon as I could. So I did as I was told and shot up the hill at such speed that even Nigel Mansell would have been proud of me. I nearly ended up in the garden at the top of the hill and it was only Mr. Foster's quick thinking as he grabbed the steering wheel, that we managed to avoid the catastrophe of ending up in my neighbour's house, let alone her garden. (I later consoled myself by thinking that other learners had done the same sort of thing. I never managed to get any evidence of that, though) I pride myself in the knowledge that during this lesson, there was one successful moment. I did manage to stop the car outside of our house.

Not with the smoothness that I was used to when I was a passenger and someone else was in the driving seat. This time I came to a standstill by stopping so suddenly that my head was thrown back, my lips felt that they were drawn back in a Richter grimace and, if I had looked in a mirror, I would probably have been the clichéd whiter shade of pale.

I was conscious of all this happening to me but hadn't given a thought to my poor driving instructor.

I turned to Mr. Foster to give my apologies and thank him for his quick reaction to my groundbreaking speed, but he was just sitting there, eyes glazed.

"Are you alright?"

Slowly his head turned towards me like a tortoise awakening from a deep sleep.

"I'm fine, thank you,"

And then, being the well-mannered gentleman that he was, he took out his filofax, and said, "Same time next week then?"

God, how I admired his courage. How many personality holes had I dug that day?

Poor, poor man. If personality was cheese, he would definitely be Gruyere by now.

For weeks and weeks I really tried my hardest to get to grips with this totally new experience, all the while wondering how it was that other people seemed to manage to drive without any problems. I consider myself to be quite intelligent, but behind the wheel another 'me' seemed to take over. A 'me' who was developing into a maniacal demon, intent in getting from a starting point to a finish in the shortest time possible, confusing other drivers with erratic signals, braking too quickly, and driving in a straight line was impossible. Instead of L plates, I should have had a sign saying, 'Don't follow me, just try another route.'

The only part of the lessons that I really took heart from was when my car managed to stagger to a stop outside of our house. I think the poor motor was so relieved at knowing it would not end up in Casualty, bandaged and plastered, that it somehow made its own way to my front door.

More practice was definitely what I needed and my husband was the only one I could think of who might, just might, be willing to sit beside me and put his life in my hands.

I was pretty dumbfounded when he allowed the 'L' plates to be fixed on to our car, but to get the 'all clear' for a lesson with him was incredible! All in all I wasn't at all offended when he added that he wouldn't drive on any actual roads with me. He was only willing to sit beside me in the passenger seat when we were out on a nearby disused airfield. This way, he could slide down in the seat and pretend he wasn't there!

An aerial view of this place would show dozens of cars reversing, driving in a straight line, driving at mysterious angles, suddenly stopping or starting. All being affected by that Kangaroo, the plague of all learner drivers. I was in my element. I was where I longed to be. My idea of a Learners Only club. A Learners only City. I drove. I reversed.

I was top of the class! I changed gears, I started the car smoothly. Everything was great.

A muffled "Not bad" from my coach from his hide-away, practically under the glove compartment, left me in euphoria! I was nearly a driver.

This elation didn't last long though because as I turned my beaming face to look at him.

I didn't notice the frenzied gesticulations of the woman at the verge – she did manage to grab her dog's collar, and I did manage to swerve out of their way!

Then I really did mess up. I had to learn the importance of 'to stop or not to stop'.

We came to a T junction. Apparently I had right of way, but hadn't learned much about this, (During my lessons I just slowed down and stopped when I was told) so when a car stopped to the right of me I stopped as well.

"What have you done that for? Drive on, you have right of way."

"It's O.K. I'll let her go first."

"Just ****** drive."

Thought – don't good manners not count then, when driving?

"Just drive." He didn't have to snarl at me like that, I was quite hurt.

As soon as it was safe, we changed places and drove home in complete silence. I was still puzzling about this whole procedure of when to give way, when to slow down etc. but when I queried it with Mr. Foster I was given a withering look and told that road safety was a priority and was then treated to a whole commentary about round-a-bouts, junctions and overtaking and to read my Highway Code. Homework I had been given weeks before.

How many times had I shouted at the kids to get their homework done, and what an example I'd set. I should have known the Highway code off by heart by now.

The need for more practice was still blatantly obvious and I managed to persuade my husband that it would be wonderful for me if he could take me out again.

Several weeks later, assuming that by now I must be getting to be a reasonable driver, he said that he would come for a drive with me. Such trust.

But hadn't he been listening to my reports of what I had done and shouldn't have done?

I'd faithfully told him of my 'progress'. I pleaded with him to give me another chance as I so needed the practice and reluctantly he did give in. He drove out of town and when there was a clear stretch of road, he pulled over and we changed places.

I was so anxious to show how good I was getting.

As I started up I did notice a rattle and asked him if he could hear it.

"It may be the door, but don't worry."

I didn't, I drove and I enjoyed myself. Not sure hubby did though as he was very quiet, but at least this time he wasn't slid down in the passenger seat. He was upright so that people could see him. He couldn't have been that ashamed of being seen with me then.

We had decided just to drive to the nearest village and I knew that there was quite a steep hill to go down so I was prepared for gear change, indicator, mirror etc. I had after all, been learning for several months, and honestly thought that I had managed to pick up some knowledge.

As we turned to the right and the downward run, my door suddenly swung open. Swinging out and then crashing back it just didn't stop! Back and fore again, and again.

I was petrified and being so used to the dual control of Mr. Foster, I took my feet off the pedals, screamed at my husband to "do something " as we freewheeled and gathered speed, down the hill, door swinging, people scattering and my husband reacting like something out of a slow motion movie. He came out of his stupor, grabbed the handbrake, turned the steering wheel, but it was too late, we had hit a stationary car.

Thankfully by then, our car had been slowed down so the impact was not as bad as it could have been.

Thoughts – too many and too confused to even remember, shaking, tears welling, hearing someone telling me that I should never apologise, b******* fool, good manners have got me into trouble again.

As my husband got back into the car, he was shaking his head.

"Poor chap has only just got his car back from a re-spray because someone had gone into the back of him last week. And now he has to take it in again."

No sympathy there then, even though I had noticed the rattle, even though I had been told it was O.K.

Forget about the 'evens', just admit to lacking in due care and attention.

Wow! She's the best

I must have been a lucrative client as my instructor drove up to collect me every week without fail, and every week I learned something new and, just as easily, I managed to forget what it was I had learned the week before. So my endeavours were at a stalemate.

What we both needed was a complete break. Me, to try and assimilate all that I was doing and him, to have the utter relief of not seeing me for a while.

He probably made a note in his Little Black Book – At last, some respite!

Well, coincidentally we both had what I thought was needed as I moved to another town. So, not only was he having a break from seeing his most faithful learner he also was never going to see me again. A lucrative pupil I may have been, but would I be missed? Not likely.

As he accepted this bit of news, I realised how wrong I had been in judging his character.

All of these months I had thought of him as a perfect gentleman. How wrong was I?

Watching his profile I could see a smile, probably one of utter relief, as he heard my words, but as he turned to face me the suspected smile had disappeared and he had composed his facial expression into one of utter regret at losing, as he put it, a dedicated driver.

Sanctimonious hypocrite! He was more than likely regretting the fact that he would no longer have a reliable source of incoming cash which I faithfully handed over weekly!

Me? I was delighted to save that weekly money and to have a valid excuse for no longer being at the wheel. I can honestly say that I didn't miss those lessons one little bit.

Then my conscience began to nag me. I had spent all that money and time on trying to learn to drive and here I was, wasting both.

Come on girl, give it another go. The battle with me and my conscience was over, I knew that if I didn't try again then I would be a loser and that I didn't want to be.

There weren't any excuses now. We'd moved, settled in, and I was working part-time so I had the time, and could afford to 'invest' in driving again. Up until now I had reverted to my old car routine - a contented passenger.

I had again got into the habit of gazing out of the window, thinking of anything but actually gripping the steering wheel, watching the traffic, changing gears etc. All of the manoeuvres that I had struggled over months and months to learn.

I shouldn't have been doing that. I should have been watching the drivers' every move then I would have kept up with all that I had been taught.

But, oh no, I didn't think I would have to be behind the wheel ever again. What a relief. This is when the battle of the conscience took over.

I shouldn't have been so complacent.

A promotion at work meant that I had to travel.

And how was I to travel?

By road. By car.

I was paranoid. Driving was haunting me and this time I couldn't escape. It was no longer some sort of hobby, it was a necessity.

I contacted another Driving Instructor.

A female Driving Instructor.

I thought that perhaps her teaching would be easier to follow and we could build up a 'sisterhood' rapport.

On my first lesson I told her, well admitted that I had had many driving lessons, which seemed to make an impression until she realised that even having spent all those hours at the wheel I was obviously not as good as I should have been. In fact when I counted up the number of lessons I had had, I should have been working towards an advanced driving certificate!

Apparently the number of lessons you need to pass your test should be equal to your age.

Well, if that's true, I must have reached 90 and still had quite a number of years to go!

I really didn't have to make any effort to prove it.

As she assessed me, she remained very calm. But what was she thinking? I wondered if she also had a Little Black Book.

Just as I had done in my previous lessons, I managed to carry on with my usual driving hiccups, but these were dealt with very competently and never, ever negatively.

Then I surprised myself.

Suddenly I was improving!

Even I realised that there was a glimmer of hope.

Things were beginning to make sense. I was actually remembering what I was supposed to do, how to do it, and when to do it.

I can only put this down to being in the care of a woman driving Instructor.

A woman.

Proof again that women were equal drivers to men.

Not only was Miss Murdoch more patient with me, but we were on the same wavelength.

Her instructions were clear, but more importantly she didn't try to push me out of my comfort zone. We worked at my pace, and at the end of every lesson, we sat in the car, and she checked that I knew what I had been doing right and what I had made a mess of. Perhaps I shouldn't generalise, perhaps there are men who are just as patient as women. Perhaps there are driving Instructors who support the principal that women can be good drivers.

Probably the training to both sexes now is the same.

I can't help thinking though, that women Instructors have more empathy.

That's an awful lot of 'perhaps' but is there some truth in them?

There wasn't any 'perhaps' though when one day, out of the blue, she said; "I think it is time now for you to put in for your test."

She wasn't asking me.

She wasn't querying it.

She was telling me.

"What?"

"We have to book a date for a driving test several weeks in advance and I think you are ready to take it."

From my very first driving lesson, the idea of taking a test, and driving on my own had fast faded.

The idea that I was going to be driving around, ferrying drunken husbands and being a Taxi service to the kids. That was a pipe dream.

I had lurched from lesson to lesson without any conscious thought of them ever going to end. I had become used to the idea that my driving was forever going to be with another Person beside me. The thought of being in the car on my own was unbelievable.

And yet here she was putting that idea into my head!

How on earth could I cope without dual controls and a professional at my side, giving me confidence, alerting me to dangers and even helping me to turn the steering wheel?

No, I wasn't ready.

I had already passed the age of 90 in driving lesson, hadn't I?

I felt that I needed to carry on until I was well past the century! Even two centuries.

But 'no' was not an option.

The forms were filled in, the date was set, all the arrangements were in place and I was on a parallel planet! This couldn't be happening to me. I really, really, wasn't geared up for it. But, it was and I just had to get motivated.

My essential bedtime reading was the Highway Code and every day I practiced The Mantra of 'Mirror, Signal, Manoeuvre' over and over again until I was brainwashed into thinking that I should do that, I could do it, and even that I would do it.

Driving test success

The nausea I had had when I was going on my first driving lesson was nothing compared to the sickness I felt on The Test morning. Spewing up all over the tester wouldn't be a good enough reason to opt out. I would just be given another date. More Vomit. Another date. And so it would go on, ad infinitum. I didn't have any alternative.

The confidence that I had managed to scrape up over all these years of learning was being totally demolished by a huge wrecking ball of panic. An even bigger lump of anxiety reared up in my throat. Caught in the crossfire was the dryness in my mouth.

My bladder had developed a leak and my hands had developed some sort of palsy.

But, here it was. It was time.

At the test centre I was escorted in by Miss Murdoch and my name was taken. It felt as if I was about to face a courtroom and a judge. My stomach was still churning, and I was quite convinced that everyone could see my legs doing a fandango of their own!

I knew that I had to get all this nervousness under control.

Thought – Mind, hands, legs all have to be working together, none of them can do their 'own thing'. Deep breaths, that's what was needed. Deep breaths and confidence is called for.

Deep breaths I could cope with but confidence, no way.

In the 90's, a written test hadn't even been thought of. Well, perhaps it had, but it was not in use and certainly not compulsory.

Perhaps if it had been, then I would probably have failed and wouldn't have gone on to take the practical test.

Instead, I was just escorted out to the car park, and into the test car by 'The Tester'.

So, the driving test began. The tester had to first ask me if I could read the number plate on the car parked the required distance away.

I must have passed on that one.

I was taking my test in a small market town, so I asked the Tester what would happen if we just happened to be held up by cattle trucks or other farm vehicles. I don't think he saw that my fingers were tightly crossed in hope! Those crossed fingers didn't do any good though because I was firmly told that the test would still take the required time, and allowance would be made for any setbacks.

"You will be given the same amount of time as required for the test to take place."

Thought – No exemption there then.

"Now, when you are ready you may start the engine."

Thought – Oh my God, this is it. I am now under test conditions.

I started the engine, put the car in gear and drove out of the car park. So that's a few things I'd done already. I'd used my eye sight, started the car, and was driving.

I relaxed a tiny bit. Miniscule really but it was definitely a bit of a boost to my ego.

My first required manoeuvre was when I was asked to turn right as we exited the car park. It will probably come as no surprise that I often confuse left and right but this time I had help. There was a No Entry sign to the left so I couldn't get that wrong.

Good start then.

As we drove along the road and I progressively changed up the gears, anxiety was vaguely fading and I even managed to convince myself that I was doing O.K.

So is my deficiency in understanding anything mechanical, proof or conjecture?

"When I slap the dashboard I want you to do an emergency stop."

To my left I could see a tractor bumping its way across the field, slowly making its way to the gate and hopefully making its way across the road in front of me. It wasn't indicating and as befuddled as I was I hoped and prayed that it would get to the gate just as I did. If I had given that farmer a bribe it would have been well worth it, because I had begun to slow down to let him out and as the book came down on the dashboard I was in first gear! What a stroke of luck. That farmer will never know the gratitude I felt for him. I never even considered that I should have been asked to make another stop. Perhaps I had a good mark for allowing the tractor to cross the road?

Mr. Tester did write something down on his clip board, and he didn't ask me to do an emergency stop again.

I managed to carry out all the necessary manoeuvres. I parked, I reversed, did the 3 point turn in 4. What an improvement on my usual number. The adrenalin must have been soaring then. I arrived in the centre of the town and another fluke. Those farmers were going to cost me a fortune in bribes! Not only had one affected my emergency stop, but by sheer fluke here they were barring my way! The cattle trucks were slowly making their way from the market and traffic was at a standstill. So we waited and waited and waited until all of the trucks began to trundle on their way, and the market place was cleared. I waited for Mr. Tester to ask me to carry on driving. Perhaps around the town again? We had been stationary for a long time, and he had told me that I was to have the set amount of time, allowances were made etc. etc. But no, I was directed back to the test centre. This was yet another fluke!

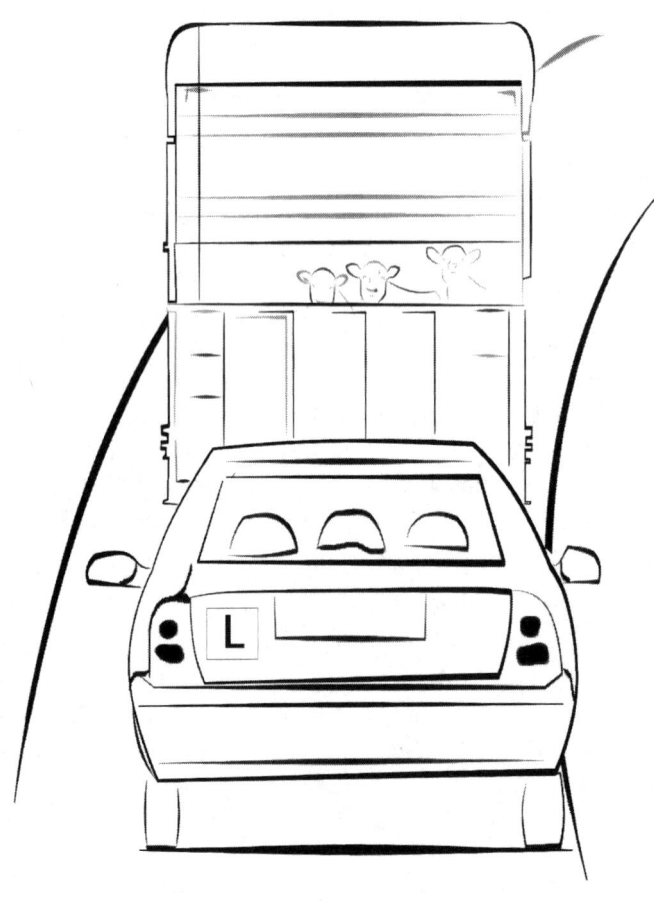

It wasn't up to me to ask any questions. I just did as I was told.

Now all I had to do was to answer 3 questions on the Highway Code and then it was all over. I can't remember what I was asked but I must have made some sort of good reply as the questioning stopped and there was silence as scribbles were made on the clip board.

I started to get out of the car when the tester stopped me

Then he pulled out an official looking form out of his briefcase.

Thought – Oh my God. I am going to have a summons. I am going to have an Endorsement on my licence and I haven't even got one yet!

"I have to ask you,"...

"What, what?"

".......if you would please sign my examiner's attendance form please."

I scrawled my name across the page and then I was off.

The car door was open, one leg was already on its way to freedom.

"Don't you want to know how you did? I have to take you through all your mistakes etc."

Thought – That will take the rest of the morning then and I'm hungry, exhausted and want to go home.

I heard "Starting with" then some technical comments and then; "So I am delighted to say that you have passed."

He was holding out the pink slip. I stared at that. I stared at him. My head bobbed as if I was giving him a curtsy, then I almost snatched that precious piece of paper, and I was out of the car. A Torpedo, a rocket, whichever missile you can think of, I was immortalised. All I could think of was escape! How the hell I had done it I'll never know, but done it, I had. First time! First time! How envious would my sons be now.

They wouldn't believe me and neither would my husband.

My legs had been shaking before the test but now they were completely locked. I had to beg Miss Murdoch, not only to drive me home but also to come in and break the news to my family.

My pink slip was scrutinized by all of the men in my life and reluctantly they had to admit that it wasn't a counterfeit. I was no longer a learner, I was a driver. I had joined that elite club at last.

I later learned that a pink slip doesn't make a good driver and my family were right – I shouldn't have passed.

No longer would I be shelling out for driving lessons.

No more asking to be driven somewhere.

Oh, no, those days were over.

Now all I had to do was drive myself, learn to fill up the car with petrol, know about tyres and oil and water and... Oh my God, How can I cope with all of that?

No, I don't want to be a driver. I can't be a driver.

Me? Behind a wheel, having control over an engine? This can't be true.

I didn't think I was capable then, and my driving proved it.

A description of my driving goes something like this – I lurched from A to B, I managed to overcome many driving fiascos, but never ever injured anyone I am glad to say.

Should I have been let loose on the roads? Probably not.

Help! I'm on the road and on my own!

"Now that I have a pink slip and I have a provisional licence, do I have to apply for a proper driving licence, or can I carry on with the one I have?"

I still couldn't believe that I had passed so was checking all the legalities before I ventured out on my own.

No, I couldn't carry on forever with the one I had.

Yes, I had forms to fill in and I had to send in my provisional and the pink slip.

That precious piece of paper that was the end result of my instructors' sweated labour and I had to give that up? I didn't want to part with it. I wanted it framed to show the world what I had achieved. So part with it I did, but when the driving licence was returned, it never had the same appeal.

All this protocol delayed the time when I was persuaded to do my first solo run.

Driving on my own was not a priority. I know it is expected that a new driver will jump into the car with confidence. I felt more like a confidence trickster. I wasn't ready yet.

Or willing to put myself in the hot seat.

The time when a newly passed driver was expected to change the 'L' for a 'P' had not yet arrived, so no-one had a clue that the woman behind or in front of them had only just passed her test. Passed her test? More a case of fooling Mr. Tester.

I was well aware of my inept driving skills, so it was a while before I had enough belief in myself to venture out on my own.

Driving solo was not a skill that I felt I had, and the men in my life certainly agreed with that. Somehow I had to prove to myself and them that I could do it.

I had to give it a try.

I had to believe that now I could get into the car, start the engine and drive off without a passenger beside me.

I was apprehensive, excited and scared to bits but I had to do it sometime, I knew, and everyone was telling me that there is nothing like getting behind the wheel without anyone criticising my technique.

But I needed someone to do that. It gave me confidence. Now the power behind the engine was under my control, and mine alone. Help!

I reluctantly got into the driving seat and had quite a conversation with myself.

Me; "Can I do this?"

Me; "Of course you can."

Me; "I don't have anyone to help me now. No one to tell me to get over a bit or to tell me that it would be better to change gear. There's so much I need help on."

Me; "But look at it positively. You can make as many mistakes as you like and no-one will be there to see."

I decided to do a small drive into town and build up my confidence slowly.

So I picked up the car keys unlocked the car, started the engine and reversed out of the car port, I drove down the road, turned left into the town, and parked.

Wow, this felt so good.

I did my shopping, went back to the car, started the engine and drove back the way I had come.

I should give a bit of road description here. From our house the road is a long gentle downward slope which then joins one of the main roads into town. This road is very steep but the distance into the town is only a few yards.

The main car park is then straight ahead, so the drive is not difficult, it just needs a bit of negotiating, especially where the two roads meet.

Driving down was fine, correct gear changes, indicating as necessary, and surprisingly I found it a very pleasant experience.

I thought that by the time I had driven down (after all, it was my first solo drive) and parked in the town, that would be my limit and I would leave the car in the car park and walk home! Then I'd get someone to collect the car later.

How stupid was that? I'd be even more of a laughing stock.

Such thoughts were quickly rejected because suddenly my confidence knew no bounds.

That should have been a warning. I was being over confident and that meant I wasn't concentrating as well as I should have been.

I thought nothing of returning to the car, starting her up and making my way home again.

Of course the return drive was very different. I had to negotiate the steep incline and of course this time the route was in reverse. This meant that I had to turn right into the gentle incline. I found this more difficult as I had to swing out a little in order to take the corner. I heard a sort of scraping noise but didn't pay it too much attention because I was concentrating on my turn, gears, mirror etc. Back up the road I drove, pleased as punch with myself.

I drove into the carport, turned off the engine and that was it. Nothing to it really. My first solo drive over and done with. My husband greeted me with the words:-

"How did you get on then?"

It was great to be able to answer, "Fine, no problem except for a strange noise when I turned to come up the road."

"What sort of noise?"

"A sort of scraping, do you think the indicator needs checking?"

"No, I think you had better check that you didn't prang another car."

Such a boost to my morale!

"Don't be daft, I would have known that, wouldn't I?"

"Not sure if you would." (Such faith!) It wouldn't hurt to check though."

As he was saying this he was making his way out to the car and examining the side back wing. He, of course, would notice the little scratch. I hadn't seen it before but who was to say that it hadn't been there for ages? Just to humour him I said that I would walk back down. I didn't see the point in taking the car out again, once was enough for that day.

I didn't want to spoil my joy.

Quite happily I wandered back down the road, but as I turned into the steep bit, I stopped in amazement. There was a big black Rolls Royce parked on the opposite side. It wasn't the parking that stopped me in my tracks, it was the sight of the long scratch along its side, showing quite clearly against the high polish.

Not only was it a Rolls Royce, it was also a hearse.

Oh my God, my first time out in the car, and it may have been me that had damaged a hearse. Did that scratch match the one on our car? Is there any way that it could be proved?

I had taken about 20 minutes to saunter down the road. I managed to get back home within 5 minutes!

Hardly able to stand up, panting, and gabbling I burst through the door, and shouted, "I've damaged the hearse, it was me, I've managed to scratch it all down its side."

"So what have you done about it?"

"Came back to tell you."

"Did you tell the funeral director what had happened?"

"No, because I don't know!"

By now, I was in an uncontrollable shake and was dumb struck. I just gazed at my husband and felt totally blank and confused. Was it me? Did I do that? Could it be proved that my car had done that, with me at wheel?

"What do I do?"

"You go back there and tell them what happened, give them your insurance details, and wait for their reaction."

"But if it wasn't me? What if it was someone else? How can anyone prove who it was?"

"Probably because there would be witnesses. Someone is bound to have seen what had happened. And, of course there is that black mark, which is obviously paint from another car."

(Why did I have to marry a copper?)

It wasn't something I wanted to do, in fact, to be quite honest, I really wanted my husband to come with me but it was obvious I was on my own with this one.

So far that morning I had driven up and down the hill, I had sauntered down the hill, I had raced like a tormented demon back up it, and now, here I was solemnly plodding down again to face up to my action.

Miserably I walked into the funeral director's office.

The receptionist looked up and gave me a sympathetic smile.

The funeral director made his way into the office, his face was heavy with condolence.

"Can we help you?"

This was it. Crunch time.

"I'm so sorry," I stuttered.

"Don't worry, take your time, we know how difficult things can be at a time like this."

Do you, do you really? I brightened up a bit at their reaction. It wasn't going to be as bad as I thought.

"It was an accident, I didn't realise the car was there."

"That must have been a great shock. Did you want to arrange the funeral now, or would you rather come back in a day or two."

Funeral What funeral? Oh my God, it suddenly dawned on me that the condolence and sympathy weren't for me but for a body, a cadaver, a corpse, someone I had driven over!

"No, no. I've come to tell you that I think I was the one who scratched the hearse."

Slowly, her smile disappeared. Condolence was wiped off his face as if by magic and in front of me stood two statues who suddenly came to life and tore past me out of the door and onto the pavement.

Two figures who one would expect to be solemn and dignified raced around the shining black vehicle and banged into each other as they discovered it. The scratch that I thought I may have been responsible for but deep down I knew, I just knew that the sound I had heard as I took the bend was me scraping this beautiful Rolls Royce car.

Now I was greeted with gritted teeth, jaws clenched, eyes on fire turning different shades of blue as anger consumed him.

"This ….is….to….be…..driven ……to a funeral, and is due to leave in 10 minutes." His voice began on a slow sonorous note, but pitched higher and higher until it was at screaming pitch.

How could I have done such a thing.

I don't like driving.

I made up my mind that this was the last time I would be behind any wheel of any car, ever.

But this heartfelt decision didn't solve this problem.

"Do I give you my insurance details now?"

It was the wrong thing to say. By now the funeral director had not only changed his facial expression, he had also changed colour.

"Leave your name and address," he hissed, his face drawing closer and closer to mine, "I will call on you later. I have a funeral to attend, and I have to draw up at the crematorium with a scratch down the side of this Rolls Royce. Just go…go…..go."

So another long walk back home. How many times that day had I been up and down the road? What sort of day had this turned out to be?

I don't like driving.

Later that day the funeral director did come to the house. Neighbours were watching as he knocked on the door. What had happened? Who had died in my family? I could almost breathe in their sympathy. How on earth could I tell them the truth?

My husband dealt with it all, and a few days later I had to write out a cheque for several hundred pounds, as all the side had to be resprayed and the car restored to its former 'see your face in it' high polish.

If this was what being in charge of the power of an engine could do, then I didn't want to have dealings with one ever again.

No escape – fate dealt me the joker

Fate had a strange way of taking charge of my life though, because a couple of weeks later I was offered a promotion. At first I was delighted until I realised that I would have to travel to my new place of work. This was in a town about 20 miles away without any form of public transport.

The only way to get there was to drive.

Oh, no, not that again!

But my guardian angel must have been looking after me because my husband was between jobs at this time and so he offered to come with me. I breathed a sigh of relief.

No driving for me then.

Not true because he was adamant that I was to be the driver and he would be the passenger. Considering his two previous experiences of driving with me, I secretly thought that this was very brave of him, but didn't dare say so.

After all, he may have forgotten those other times, and who was I to remind him?

I consoled myself with the fact that at least I would have company in the car and also some help if I should do anything wrong. Plus there were no funeral parlours on that route just lovely open moorland and a quiet road.

For several months this worked out very well until the day came when my husband did get a job and then I was on my own

Thought – Here I go again.

That first morning I started off with very little confidence and doing about 20 m.p.h. I figured out that the slower I went, the less likely I was to have an accident.

I hadn't reckoned with all the other drivers who were in a hurry to get to work and wanted to overtake me. With all the bends and dips in this quiet road I had never realised that there were quite so many cars using it. That was because I had been doing a decent speed and had a competent passenger to advise me.

Not so on this drive.

Now, every time I glanced in my rear view mirror I could see another car, or lorry, bearing down on me.

In my nervous state of mind I likened them to big brutes and they were after me. Big black horns charging at me, huge clouds of steam blowing from their nostrils. Pawing at ground behind my back , ready to heave me out of their way if necessary.

And that was just the cars! The lorries, in my fevered imagination were dinosaurs.

They weren't just going to heave me out of the way, they were going to either toss me on to the moor or worse still trample me underfoot.

As these monsters tore past me, I breathed a sigh of relief, but as the journey went on, the sighs developed into a muted choking as I gulped in huge mouthfuls of air.

It was the pawing of the hooves that was tormenting me, once they had gone I sort of relaxed until the next brute appeared.

How I got to work that day I don't remember. What I do remember is my manager asking to speak with me a couple of hours later.

"What's the problem?"

"Your car."

Thought – Not again. What had I done wrong this time?

"We thought we had better move it for you. Can I have your keys."

"What have I done this time?"

Trying to hide his superior smile, his answer surprised me.

"It's because you have parked about a centimetre from the outside fire escape."

"Yes, I know, it was the only place I could find this morning." What was he on about?

"Yes, but when you start her up you are bound to move forward ever so slightly and then you will be totally bang in the middle of the ironwork, and there will be a hell of a job trying to get you out. The only thing we can do is gently release the handbrake and push it back a bit. We only hope we can do it."

He waited expectantly, I suppose for some sort of response, but I was dumbstruck. I thought I had parked beautifully, I had coped with all those beasts chasing me, and now here I was, in trouble again.

"I didn't realise that I was so close."

I fetched my keys and left them to it. Very churlish I must admit, but me and the patronising attitude of the male members of the staff didn't really gel very well.

I should have shown gratitude, I should have even gone with them to see what they meant. Instead I hurried back to work and took shelter in my room. I couldn't do any damage there, could I? Well for starters…no, I won't even think about it.

Every day I had to face up to the myth that continuous driving would increase one's capability and confidence. Not so.

But I had to keep going and gradually over the weeks I did manage to improve a little.

I no longer parked incorrectly. I wasn't going to give my male colleagues the satisfaction of having to move my car out of a dire situation. Oh no, I made sure that I got to work early and parked in an easy space. One that allowed me to reverse without hitting any other car and was then facing the correct way to exit the car park.

I gradually came to terms with the other drivers on the road. I would go a bit faster (within safety speeds of course) if they wouldn't breathe so heavily down my neck.

It was all going so well that I even offered to take my son to college.

I was glowing with confidence. I had company. I had passed my test the first time He had had to take his twice.

As we were driving along, I noticed him glancing over at me and at my hand on the gear stick. He's taking it all in, I thought, he's realising that his Mum is a good driver after all.

After a little while he said, "Mum, why did you change gear then?"

"Because I always change into that gear on this bit of road."

It was a long time before he stopped laughing and it is still the bit he loves to tell everyone when he describes the first time he went out in our car with me at the wheel.

The bit when I admitted that I had definite gear change land marks. Regardless of speed or manoeuvres, I changed gear at that point.

So for many weeks I drove all over the place and most of the journeys were without too many problems. I was beginning to have quite a list of incidental bumps and scratches like managing to get the wing mirror caught on a farm gate as I turned to go out on the road. I also remember reversing into a bollard on one occasion, bumping into the car in front of me when we had to stop at some traffic lights on another, but I didn't hit it hard enough to do any damage. I was aware though that my husband's patience was wearing a bit thin, as by now, I was beginning to build up quite a few 'insurance claims'.

Well, not really claims. If I had tried to make claims for all of the bumps, scratches and bangs, our premium would be rocketing up. So I kept a secret hoard of cash locked away, anything I did I could then pay for. Good ploy. No insurance claims for me, I had a clean record, even if I did probably pay out twice as much as any insurance firms.

On a daily basis, unlike many husbands, mine no longer asked me if I had had a good, good day at work. I was usually greeted with "So what have you done today?"

Referring to the car, not my actual work.

Sometimes I found this quite hurtful, as there were days when I had driven perfectly, but he was never that convinced. I consoled myself with the thought that everyone has a bit of a problem with their driving at one time or another, don't they?

Every time I bumped, scratched or stalled the car I kept telling myself that I could only get better and in spite of my dislike of being at the wheel I did persevere.

So, thinking that I had experienced every kind of minor accident that was possible, I wasn't prepared for the next predicament that I managed to get myself into.

On this occasion I decided to take a drive onto the moors so that I could give our dog a good long run. Of all the many walking areas on the moor, I went and chose the one that was a bit off the beaten track. A very pretty walk beside one of the many streams that criss-crossed across the open moorland.

I can well remember that wonderful feeling of freedom and the thought of a stress free couple of hours. How wrong was I. The place I chose to park was miles away from where the usual visitors stopped. Those huge car parks which are usually full of mainly empty cars. Abandoned by their drivers, they gave an air of misery and neglect mournfully waiting for the return of the humans who had deserted them in favour of traipsing over this untamed terrain. Not all of them are empty though. There are a fortunate few whose drivers will not leave them. Those drivers and their passenger (there is usually only one) who park up and sit for hours, staring at the turf stretching far into the distance, as if they can conjure up some magical event to tell their friends. That would sound so much better than telling the story of how they parked up on the moors, sat for hours gazing at the heather, bracken and turf in some sort of glazed reverie, and then drove home again

So my parking spot was quiet, in fact it wasn't even a car park, just the grass verge.

I parked the car, the dog was on his lead, wellie boots were on, (me, not the dog) and we set off. After a good long walk we plodded wearily back to the car and I slumped on the driving seat for a well earned rest.

Breath back, energy restored, time to go home. I put the key in, started the engine, put her into reverse gear, released the handbrake, foot on the accelerator, and nothing.

I tried again. Foot on the accelerator, engine roaring, nothing.

I had enough sense to check the dashboard but there were no warning lights flashing. The only lights flashing were in my head. Oh, my God!

Help! We were out in the wilds, so how on earth could I get anyone to sort me out?

All of this happened in those primitive days before mobile phones had even been thought of. I was on my own.

My relaxing few hours, and the stress free time I had envisaged had been and gone. I tried not to panic as I realised that there wasn't even a telephone box out here.

The familiar red box that looked like Dr. Who's Tardis with a link to people via a black handset. Then I realised that even if I did find one, I didn't have any coins to put in so that I could be given a connection. And who would I phone? Not 999, not emergency.

How could I admit to being stuck out on the moors when I had a car parked right beside me?

The only solution would be for me walk down the road a bit then I might find some cottages with nice kind people who would welcome me in, make me a cup of tea, and sort out the mess I had got myself into. But I hadn't driven past any houses or cottages on the way here. It would mean going further on but all I could see was miles and miles of moorland.

No, I had to face it. I was in a mess and I was on my own. Except for my dog of course, and she was curled up on the back seat, snoring her head off, and completely oblivious to my panic.

And by now I was panicking. How was I to get home? There must be a way that I could get the car to go. But nothing would budge it. Not even swearing, banging on the boot, kicking the tyres. All of that helped my frustration, but wasn't any good for the car.

Perhaps it just had a cob on?

I tried the gentle approach. But talking to it didn't help either.

Thought – Be rational.

Thoughts What options do I have here? First of all someone may pass by?

Thought – Very unlikely all the way out here. Second option would be to start to walk home and hope that I managed to get some sort of help, phone, person, etc.

Thought – I may meet a passing breakdown truck – this thought just showed how hysterical I was getting.

A break down truck would only arrive if I phoned for one, which I couldn't, or if they were on their way to another car catastrophe. Strangely, the thought of other people getting stuck on the moors gave me a bit of comfort. But that solace didn't last long. I had to put a check on myself and think practically.

Thought – None of these options were realistic and I resigned myself to having to stay in the car overnight and just wait until I was missed at home, and then a search party would be organized to find me.

I would be the centre of attention. I had visions of helicopters flying overhead, whilst I waved frantically to gain their attention. Because I was tired, hungry and stressed out, my mind began to twin with the car – out of gear!

I comforted myself by switching on the radio, and at least I had my dog to protect me, even if she was snoring her head off and doing that funny "rabbit chasing" twitch as she dreamt in total oblivion of the situation I, or rather, we were in.

By the time I had had an hour or so of listening to various radio programmes I was beginning to calm down a bit.

I have to say that at the time I didn't realise how lucky I was to even have a radio to listen to! My situation on that day was more geared to the old sort of 'seek' station radio that was around in the 1950's. Those car radios had two switches, named Town and Country. I was in the country but didn't have the pedal on the floor to tune in to that type of station. The pedal activated the tuner, which then stopped the motor.

I wasn't in the 1950's though, seeking a Town or Country station, and having the motor stop to tune in, I was stuck out on the moor! No, I was listening to soothing music on a push button radio and never even gave a thought to the possibility that this would make the battery flat.

Calming myself down wasn't going to get me home though. I needed assistance and I needed it fast. I was getting hungry, thirsty and cold.

Now and then I had tried to get the car to move but each time it was telling me "No way."

In the distance I thought I heard an engine of some sort, but as I had the music on practically full volume, Concorde could have flown over and I would barely have heard.

But an engine there was.

My angel. My rescuer! Not exactly a prince on a white charger, just a working farmer on an old but obviously trustworthy tractor.

The astonishment on his face when he saw me is still etched in my memory.

Well, who wouldn't be astonished at the sight of a possibly insane creature standing in your way, waving her arms like a windmill and trying to shout over the noise of a tractor.

I can only thank him for stopping and be even more grateful for his help. When he got off the tractor I began to babble all about the car and how it wouldn't start and how I didn't know how I was going to get home... Suddenly I realised that he was staring at me, I stopped in mid-sentence and used my very best pathetic look.

I am ashamed to admit to all feminists that I played up the 'little woman in distress' bit. But what else could I do? I had already proved that I wasn't thinking or acting like a mechanic, male or female. At this particular time, I looked as I genuinely felt.

Totally stressed.

"Well, then, my love, I'd better take a look at 'un then, hadn't I?"

"Please," I begged, "yes, please." I would have got on my knees if it had helped.

By now he must have realised that I was not insane, just overwrought as I explained my problem, this time with less shouting and more information, and he got into the car and tried to put it into reverse. I'm glad to say that it didn't work for him either.

Glad because I had tried that and it hadn't worked for me either, but I also felt very humbled that he was being such a kind Samaritan.

His long working day had been made even longer by me.

I had completely disrupted his day but, although he appeared quite calm, I'm sure that the amount of swearing that he was thinking couldn't be spoken out loud.

Not in front of a lady. A lady who didn't know the first thing about mechanics.

I realised that once again I was failing my driving sisters. Those stalwart women who had had to learn everything about a car's 'insides' during the war!

I thought I was stupid, he was probably mentally describing me as, bleep, bleep, bleep woman, in fact I don't know how many bleeps he could have managed, and they wouldn't have been blue, but deep purple.

He got out of the car and gave it a long stare, then he took off his greasy cap.

Thought – Why is it that when a man is puzzled by something, he always takes his hat off and scratches his head?

He walked all round the car, flattening even more grass than I had already. I had done the same so many times that it resembled a circle in a corn field.

Now he did what I had failed to do. He bent down and looked underneath I stood there transfixed. Don't tell me that the bottom of the car had dropped off, pleeeeeeease!

"Well, you've done a good job here then, haven't you?"

"Have I?"

"You've only been and parked yourself on a damn great boulder!"

"But I parked on the grass verge."

"Yes, and in the grass there is a great big granite boulder. Didn't you feel anything when you parked up?"

"No, not a thing, and I wasn't expecting to neither. It just looked like long grass to me."

By now, I was beginning to get a bit irate. I'd been here for ages, I was hot and thirsty and here he was telling me that I should have known that I had parked on a sodding great stone!

I felt like asking him if he would have done the same thing, but then thought better of it as he probably wouldn't have (being a man, he wouldn't admit to it anyway) Also, at this moment in time I needed all the help I could get so it was not the time to get on my high horse but time to docilely accept my stupidity and accept everything he told me.

After crawling around under the car for a little longer, he came up for air and told me he would have to get the tractor and tow me off. I had to get into the car, release the handbrake when he said and leave the rest to him.

This latter instruction, well order really, he said in a very serious tone and a grim face - he was obviously not at all hopeful that I could do this simple task.

I got into the car and waited. There was a lot of movement going on at the rear of the car and then the tractor engine started and a voice bellowed, "Let her go," and I did, and the car suddenly shot back and off its resting place. Probably with some relief I suspect.

"Handbrake on!" the voice bellowed again.

I got out of the car and thanked him so much. How could I have done it without him etc. etc., and I did sincerely mean every word. So the towing rope was removed, I was back in the driving seat and he made sure the engine fired before he chugged off to do what he was going to do before he had the pleasure of meeting me, stranded and hysterical.

Perhaps I ought to mention here that my dog was still half awake on the back seat, her eyes half open at the sound of the hollering and shouting and then closing gently as she slowly slipped back into her dream world of bones, walkies and rabbits.

Having started the engine, I slowly made my way home, hoping against hope that the poor car wouldn't suddenly go into trauma and stop suddenly. Thankfully there were no problems apart from a pretty loud clanking. Not surprising really, the poor thing was probably in its death throes.

As I drove along I thought of the film Casablanca when Humphrey Bogart greets Katherine Hepburn with the line "Of all the gin joints in all the world you have to walk into mine," only in my case it was "Of all the boulders in the whole of Dartmoor you have to bloody well have to perch on that one."

In 2005, I read that near the village of Belstone on Dartmoor, a granite boulder had been dedicated to the Poet Laureate, Ted Hughes. For a moment my heart missed a beat. Was this 'my' boulder. Singled out for fame at last and not because my car had been a see-saw on it? No, it wasn't that boulder, but one that had been air lifted into place by the private helicopter of Prince Charles'. Just for one fleeting moment I thought that I had achieved notoriety and could honestly say "I was there first." But I wasn't.

My friend at the garage (we were on the best of terms) told me that I had damaged the sump, whatever that is, but apparently it is important, so my sympathy towards the poor cars death throes was proved to be true.

One of these days I will get done for car slaughter, and following that my husband will be done for manslaughter (woman slaughter).

Then we bought a new car. That wasn't the end of my 'boulder one' though because a few weeks later to my horror our neighbour drove home in it, and was so obviously pleased with his bargain that we couldn't admit the state it was in when we exchanged it for another model.

We did wonder if he knew anything about the problem with the sump? Surely the garage would have sorted it out before it was sold?

The balancing act, the sump, the sale, all of these must have taken their toll on the poor thing.

And it did die.

The battery caught fire and it was a write off, cremated and sent off to car heaven.

How could I have treated it so badly but there was no time to grieve.

I had yet another car to break in.

Oh no, not again!

A Red Metro replaced the 'sump' car.

A brand new one.

Was my husband insane? Allowing me loose on the roads with a brand new car?

I wasn't happy with it.

I took an instant dislike to it.

I found it was difficult to steer and kept pulling to the left.

I don't have a lot of strength in my arms. Any person (man) who says that's because I am a woman, will soon be faced with a whole army of angry females, so be warned.

I found the Metro very difficult to hold steady but according to the man in my life there weren't any problems. As far as he was concerned it was very easy to control.

In other words 'don't make excuses with this car."

But my assessment was an honest one. It did have steering problems. I was right.

And this was to be proved at a later date.

My daily drive was still over the moors, but now I was driving in the opposite direction. Not because of any geographical lapses of memory, merely due to the fact that my workplace had changed.

I know that I have a problem with left and right, but even I knew which way I had to drive to work. I am proud to say that I never, never, drove out of the drive and went left instead of right. I conditioned the car to know when I may have had a bit of a blip by promising it a lovely soapy shampoo. It never got it. Things moved too swiftly for that!

The first week or so I was fine.

It was during the summer so traffic was pretty heavy and most of the time I was in first or perhaps second gear as the traffic was practically bumper-to-bumper with all the commuters. I was perfectly happy in the queue. I wasn't the one who honked and swore in frustration. This was my kind of driving and I loved it.

Then down came the rain.

I haven't suddenly gone off the topic of my driving abilities and started a career as a weather forecaster, but driving conditions, when driving, are important and need to be adjusted to.

So it was raining and the roads were a bit greasy.

I know all this because my husband had warned me of the difficulties of driving in these conditions and to take care. So I was aware of problems.

I set off, and a little while later my husband set off on his motorbike.

He drove along the road, negotiated the round-a-bout leading to the moor and a little way along he saw out of the corner of his eye the back of a Red Metro sticking out from the depths of the moorland

Now, as an ex-policeman my husband is very observant, and even though he was riding a bike and the car was half buried in the gorse bushes he knew our number plate.

He pulled over and gaped at the sight of me struggling out of the car.

"What the hell have you gone and done now?"

"It wasn't my fault, I tried to slow down. But couldn't hold the wheel as it pulled to the left."

You know the word 'disparaging'? Well that is a wonderful description of his face at that moment in time

He didn't rant and rave. Probably because he was resigned to my compulsion to engage in road disaster.

He just got off his bike, sat in the car, put it into reverse, manoeuvred it out of the gorse bush and onto the grass verge ready for me to drive off.

Not a word was spoken. He then got on to his bike and went on his way.

I was so full of admiration for my man.

But the car – I am quite sure it was smirking at me but well aware that it couldn't argue, the surge of male testosterone it had just succumbed to made it very amenable.

Huh!

Getting back into the driving seat I managed to make it into work but never admitted to anyone the real reason as to why I was a bit (well a lot) late. I just put it down to the volume of traffic, and everyone believed me.

Again.

God, how I hate driving.

In my defence there was an article in the national newspaper a few months later stating that there was a design problem with Metro's. It had been discovered that the steering was veering to the left.

How chuffed was I? See. It wasn't all my fault then, was it? I felt like standing on the roof of the red devil, forcefully shouting;-

I TOLD YOU SO.

So we changed the car again. The idea was, that this would prevent me from having a proper accident.

We shouldn't have done that.

An accident was already looming on the horizon ready to pounce.

You can't argue with a hunt

I can't believe that my husband actually went ahead and bought another brand new car! Was he masochistic or something?

This time it was a Silver Fiesta which I had to drive back and forth to work.

Why, oh why, couldn't we have had an old banger that I could have knocked about to my heart's content and not worry about any scratches, bangs, smashed mirrors etc. I would have been delighted with one like that, but, oh no, we had to have another brand new one.

Bad decision.

I have to admit though, that I did like driving this car. I'll say that again, "I did like driving that car," because this was the first time that I had felt like that. It was smooth, it was easy to drive and I really knew that it liked me.

We bonded.

I should have known it was too good to be true. Most of my 'incidents' happened, for some reason, when I was on my way to somewhere, but this time I was on my way home when the incident occurred. I don't seem to have a particular time of day though, when I become dysfunctional. It can happen at any time.

It was still summer and once again a lovely sunny day. For a change the traffic was light, and I was, in my mind, driving fantastically. I had the window open and was in a wonderful world. Sun, music, warm air. I had the window wound right down, and the cassette player on pretty loud. C.D. players, I-pods, air conditioning, satnavs, mobile phones, etc were all still at the design stage, but we did have radios and cassette players.

So there was I, singing and driving, without a care in the world.

As I came over the brow of the hill, I had a good clear view of the road as it stretched across this beautiful part of the country. What more could anyone want.

Way, way down the road I saw that the hunt was out, hounds were milling all over the road as their whipper-in was trying to get them to follow the scent of the fox, not to chase after any other fantastic moorland whiffs that their keen noses discovered.

(This was in the days before the Prohibition of Fox Hunting Act so it was a real animal) I was impressed at the sight of the riders in their hunting pink, the gorgeous horses and the working hounds.

Looking at this panoramic view ahead didn't affect my driving however I slowed down, knowing that eventually all traffic would have to come to a halt. Hunts are renowned as the cause of traffic having to wait or swerve to avoid horses and riders, plus the hounds.

So I was feeling quite complacent with my response to the conditions ahead.

As I slowed down I checked my mirror and the road behind was clear.

A few minutes later my reverie was shattered.

I found myself being hurled forward.

What the hell was that?

I had been cannoned into by a maniac (not me this time!) who was driving too fast and had zoomed over the brow of the hill. It had cannoned into me with such force that I barely had time to react.

I had the presence of mind to try and steer to the left as I fleetingly remembered that if I hit the car in front I would be in trouble regardless of the circumstances. But because of my previous careful driving I had left the maximum space between me and the car in front so I merely touched the grass verge before stopping with a juddering halt.

Shaking like a leaf I emerged from my car. By now three cars were stationary.

The one behind me had no choice. Smoke was coming out of it and the front was pretty crushed. I was on the grass verge and the driver who had been in front of me had pulled in to the side of the road.

He made his way over and helped me onto the grass until I had calmed down and had stopped shaking. By now someone had notified the police, or they may have been on duty with the hunt, I don't know, but a constable did appear and started to take down details. I have no idea what had happened to anyone else. I was too dazed even to notice who had driven into me.

I just remember thinking "it wasn't my fault, just for once it wasn't my fault. If this is what driving with due care and attention means then I would rather go back to my other method."

Glancing over at my poor Fiesta, the love of my life, I was desperate to check her out, although she looked perfectly fine.

Thought – After that huge crash the car wasn't harmed at all!

Then I looked around the other side.

Oh my God! The front driving seat was practically facing the other way. The back tyre was off, There were buckles and dents everywhere.

"What will my husband say," I wailed. "This is our new car."

"Well, it certainly wasn't your fault."

In my dazed state that sounded like an echo of my own voice.

I was still puzzling out the stereo effect when fate stepped in.

Suddenly an ambulance, appeared, reversed back, and stopped right beside me.

Apparently the crew had been on their way back to base and hadn't expected to see such a scene as they crested the hill.

"How are you feeling love?" Concerned faces were staring down at me.

"Fine."

"No cuts or bruises?"

Thought – it isn't me who has been crushed and beaten it's my poor car. She needs seeing to by my garage doctor, not me.

"I think you'd better get into the ambulance and we'll take you to the hospital for a check-up."

This startled me.

"I'm fine, really I am."

But they wouldn't take no for an answer, and I had to go, leaving my beautiful damaged car neglected and sorry for itself by the roadside.

All these years later I have no idea how the car was moved to a garage, how my husband turned up at the hospital, and certainly don't remember any medical examination. I just remember sitting on the settee at home wearing a neck collar to help with any whiplash injury I might.

The emptiness of our driveway was a continuous reminder that my sleek silver friend was badly injured trying to protect me from a bad injury.

It was a very emotional day when I went to visit my beautiful Fiesta. I was in tears when I saw it huddled in the garage where it had been towed after the accident.

It was so obviously a write off.

As my husband looked at the damage his face was a picture.

"How the hell did you get out of that? You could have been crippled for life, if not killed."

As far as I know the driver who had caused the damage wasn't charged. I never had to appear in court anyway. But, to be honest, I didn't care. I was bereaved.

The insurance claim went through, and we had yet another new car. A Peugeot.

If I thought that my husband was masochistic when he bought the Fiesta, I now had proof that he was stark, staring bonkers.

This was the last straw.

I had now used up so many cars I knew that I could not commit any more murders.

My driving career had started by me scraping a hearse, and it finished by me practically ending up in one!

The parting of the ways

I remember so well sitting in the driving seat on my very first lesson, dreaming of years of endless hours spent at the wheel of a car, enjoying the freedom, the ability of going to my chosen destinations whenever, and wherever I desired.

When did that dream explode into a nightmare?

If I am honest, the nightmares started when I first sat myself in that driving seat!

Admittedly I did staunchly carry on and overcame so many obstacles that at times I did think that I wasn't such a manic driver after all, and then along would come another 'incident' and it was a case of "Here I go again."

Hadn't I tried to bond with all of my cars? Was it because a close relationship had never really blossomed? It never developed from a tiny need to a full on passion?

I have to admit that the cars I had driven never appeared to be that crestfallen when we had to part company. There was no begging for me to be again at the wheel once more.

I don't think that any of them felt particularly bereft or betrayed when it all ended.

And can anyone blame them?

Over the years I'd been driving, all of them had suffered at some time or other at my hands.

All of them at some time had had to be taken to the garage for a variety of repairs.

Ranging from that one write-off when I had been entangled with the hunt, all the way down to a broken side mirror.

We always used the same garage, and the response became automatic when the current car of ours limped into the forecourt with me in control, well sort of.

Like paramedics rushing out to the patient with life preserving equipment and stretcher at the ready, so the mechanics raced out to greet the two of us. Not with concerned faces though, just great guffaws as each one tried to guess why I was visiting them this time!

What repair did the crestfallen vehicle need this time? Had I run out of water again?

Was she scratched, bumped, dented? All three? Or something entirely new. Some part of her bodywork that so far had managed to escape the ravages and lesions that I had inflicted on the rest of the framework.

Where, oh where, were women mechanics? They would have been more empathetic.

Anyone would think I was a regular visitor. I didn't drive in every week. There was often months in between visits. If I had been at the garage that frequently surely they would have brought my tea in my own special mug wouldn't they? No doubt if I had offered to bring one they would have accepted it without even a raised eyebrow.

There were times when I had only scratched the paintwork ever so slightly. Then it wasn't in need of any desperate attention which disappointed my 'friends' and meant that I would be treated without any ceremony. My cars didn't need patching up continuously, any little scratches would be sorted out when I had to go in for a bigger bump.

One thing was certain though, the costs were mounting up. Our Motor Insurance had a mysterious way of doing a disappearing act when needed. I did ask at one point if there was any way that the policy could help me out but was told pretty adamantly that the 'no claims' clause was not to be touched. So, that meant I had to re-adjust my budget and carry on including a 'car repairs when necessary' column.

If I had had the nerve to take out my own Insurance Policy and claimed for every little misdemeanour I'd have to own up to, every single Insurance company would black-list me. I would join the club of 'impossible to insure' members.

From all parts of Great Britain the word would spread like wild fire.

If computers were around then attempting to fool them by going on line wouldn't have been any good and gocompare.com would flag up 'This internet page is not available' at that particular moment."

I had to face the facts that I was doomed.

I had to pay all the costs.

My cars lost out, my budget lost out, the only people who benefited were the garage crew!

Because I was such a good cash customer, the speedy way that all the scratches, dents, bumps, breakages etc. were dealt with was admirable. So quick that very few people knew. Hardly anyone else knew about my crap driving.

Unless they were with me, of course.

Strangely enough, this didn't happen very often, as I rarely gave anyone a lift.

I didn't need to anyway, as I mainly worked from home, driving to my clients, and only went into the main office once a week.

So on what I like to call my 'garage visit days' I would leave home, go on several house calls, challenging my car to cope with the sport of giving another car a close shave.

If it managed to survive this then it was asked to dodge overhead branches, or divert itself from hitting farm gates. I asked so much of the poor vehicle because it knew its reward. Being forsaken on the garage forecourt yet again.

Cheerfully I would park up, walk home, wait for the call to tell me that the wound was healed by using all the tools and stuff that mechanics store, and all I had to do then was walk back, pay the bill and drive home. There wasn't a time when I took it in, collected it and then had to take it in again. The drives home from the garage always seemed to be accident free. Perhaps that was because the car was a nervous wreck and miraculously managed the drive to its home in one piece. All of my cars were not addicts or neurotics.

They didn't enjoy all the attention they had to endure in the workshop. Having their bonnet lifted was bad enough, but when a strange person had to fiddle around underneath, then that was humiliation. And how did I repay their loyalty? By embarrassing them time and time again.

As I am in confessional mode there is another aspect that I should confess.

I have trouble with recognising left and right.

I found that I had to really concentrate on using the correct indicator.

Sometimes I totally confused a following vehicle as the driver tried to work out why my indicators were doing a dance of their own, as they flashed from left to right and back again. I became an expert at ignoring the furious honk and the rude gestures made by the irate driver, who obviously didn't appreciate my flashing. Indicators that is!

I did learn from their reaction though, because I then worked out a good strategy. If I used the left hand signal, then that is the way I would turn. The same if I signalled right.

Perfect.

This meant that there wasn't any confusion to the driver behind. He or she went on their way not realising the sacrifice that I had made for them. I had managed to turn a simple manoeuvre into a big problem. Quite a big problem as it happened, because by following the choice I had made when I indicated I managed to go completely in wrong directions.

But I managed to sort myself out quite easily.

As we live in a rural area, there was usually a lane where I could practice my three point or four or five point turn and get back onto my original route, and then turn in the correct direction, the one I should have chosen in the first place. If I had a passenger in the car then I could always make the excuse that I had gone the wrong way, or I often asked them to check that I was driving in the right direction.

This meant that if I did use the wrong indicator I could put the blame on them!

This left/right hand confession may also help to clear up the mystery of why my cars were so accident prone. Smashed wing mirrors, dents etc. were usually par for the course when I had to turn, as this usually had to be in the gateway of a field. The lanes were too narrow to turn in, even I knew that.

So, having sorted out how I could rectify my wrong turn ability I began to relax a bit more when I knew a turn was coming up. The agitation which I had suffered at those awful apparitions I could see in my rear view mirror, those scowling faces, gradually disappeared, and as normality was resumed, I became quite laid back. Turning in the wrong direction, changed from being a common occurrence, to an occasional 'one off'. The sighs of relief from my driving 'sisters' is almost tangible because I was no longer creating a 'damned women drivers' situation.

Again and again, I was guilty of putting all women drivers at risk of being known as 'Female catastrophes' at the wheel.

Again and again, I had to struggle to try and make sure that I managed somehow to cover up all my dreadful mistakes, and I became quite good at it. I often managed to fool my family when I'd made a cock up.

Like the time my left/right ability was at an all time high.

It was when I was making a night drive. There wasn't any problem in arriving, it was just the drive home that went wrong. I have to say that there wasn't any drink involved. I have never, ever drunk alcohol before getting into a car as a driver.

I shudder to think of such a double whammy. Me and drink? God forbid. I'm bad enough sober!

I cheerfully left my meeting, so happy in my little car world. Oblivious to the hazard I was about to fall right into.

I signalled as I drove out of the car park, for a change going the right way. I thought.

By now, our cars had been updated and there were radios fitted! So there I was, singing along, checking the mirrors, changing gears, and being a creditable driver.

Lost in this wonderful world of happiness, it was a while before I realised that I was being passed by an awful lot of cars. I should have been on a quiet country road, where the only cars to pass me would be the usual ones who couldn't stand driving behind anyone going at less than 40 miles an hour, tops.

Then it dawned on me, that in fact I had taken the wrong turn, and was now on a dual carriageway. I usually avoided those like a plague. They meant overtaking, and having to drive at speed.

My nerves began to boil up into heebie-jeebies. I was on a dual carriageway!

I had done it again, I had turned left instead of right. I was gaily heading towards the city!!

Talking to myself was the norm when I was in the car and trying to sort out what I should be doing. But now I was lost for words. Stunned. Bewildered. How the hell do I get home now?

There was no country lane to rescue me. I was on my own.

Cars whizzed past and my speed gradually became more and more erratic as I tried to figure out what I should do. The only thing in my favour was that I didn't come to a standstill. At least I knew that wouldn't be the way out.

Then my headlights lit up a road sign. One that was familiar. If I made it on to that road then I was O.K. I nearly blew myself home with my sigh of relief. All I had to do was concentrate on indicating and turning.

I did it, and by making the right detour I was so relieved when I parked outside our house.

As I wandered into the lounge, my husband looked up from the telly;-

"You're home later than I expected. I hope you haven't had another prang?"

In all honesty I was able to say "No."

It wasn't very long after this that we decided to go and live in Cyprus and when we saw the standard of driving over there both of us made the mutual decision that this was not, definitely not the place for me to risk any more driving. Conditions in Cyprus would not allow me to take any more risks. To leave myself open for any sort of 'incident'. Any problems I encountered would more than likely lead to a fatality in that country, so thanks but no thanks.

My dislike of driving had run its full course.

I had endeavoured to join the driving elite. I had done my best. But best was not good enough.

Certainly not good enough to show all the fantastic women drivers that I could be like them. No, all that I had managed to do was to keep alive the idea that women drivers were always the ones who were at fault. I was the exception, not the rule.

The rule is that women are better drivers than men. Insurance companies say so, and there is historical evidence.

Wars, social class, chauvinistic attitudes.

Nothing has put women off from their goal of being accepted as great drivers.

Over the decades they've been inspired by their fantastic female ancestors who have shown, by their example, how to succeed.

I'm not sure what the descendants of Violette Morris would have thought of her example though.

Racing in the 1920's, Violette had a double mastectomy so that she could be as close to the driving wheel as her male competitors.

I think that women would agree that that is taking equality just a bit too far!

But to Genevra, Violette and women drivers everywhere, I know when I am beaten. I can no longer embarrass you all.

I quit.

I never got to drive on a motorway, or use an automatic, or use a 5th gear. But not to worry, once more the roads are safe.

I can give one quote though which I think is applicable -

'A critic is a man who knows the way but can't drive the car.' (Kenneth Tynan)